H O R S E   F E V E R

HORSE FEVER

by William Murray

DODD, MEAD & COMPANY

NEW YORK

Second Printing

Library of Congress Cataloging in Publication Data

Murray, William, date
    Horse fever.

    1. Horse-racing—Personal narratives.   2. Murray,
William, date   I. Title.
SF335.5.M87   798'.4'00924 [B]   76-12532
ISBN 0-396-07336-0

This book is dedicated to the memory
of Hal Scharlatt, a fine editor and
a loving friend. He is much missed.

Contents

*Some of my favorite performers
are horses!*
—Frank Sinatra

H O R S E   F E V E R

1

Where the Turf Meets the Surf

I drove south with the horses. We didn't all leave at the same time, of course. The big vans had been moving down the freeways for days, from as far north as San Francisco and the fair circuits of central and northern California, though most of them had been loading up at Hollywood Park, where the long spring and early-summer race meeting was at last coming to a close. Yes, the Thoroughbreds and the men and women who lived and died by them were headed now for the new scene of action at Del Mar, a pretty little track on the coast about twenty miles north of San Diego, and I was going with them. I left my house in Santa Monica on the morning of July 22, 1975, the day before the start of the Del Mar meeting, and on the way down, weaving in and out of the usual thick traffic along the San Diego Freeway, I passed several of the vans monopolizing the slower right-hand lanes. I felt like waving and cheering, but I didn't. Perhaps it was because I

suspected I wasn't yet a professional in this business, not
really on the inside of the game, but just another horse de-
generate, after all, heading south for a summer of self-
indulgence.

It was a trip I'd been wanting to make for years. What
could be better, I asked myself, than spending a whole
racing season somewhere just basking in the sun, writing
a bit in the morning and picking winners in the afternoon?
Especially not near any large city, but in some isolated
place where I'd be able to mingle with the horse people,
live and die with their fortunes daily, and maybe party a
little with them at night. My idea of paradise! Before I
moved to California from New York in the mid-sixties, I'd
dreamed, for instance, of passing the four weeks of every
August at Saratoga, where the racing then (and maybe
even now) is still conducted in the leisurely atmosphere
of a small resort town, but I was never able to get away.
Work, a wife, children, responsibilities—all the traditional
obstacles to pure pleasure always stood in my way. I
escaped to the track whenever I could, on weekends especially and on afternoons snatched from the treadmill of
literary hustling. (Wasn't it Voltaire who said you could
make a man with children do anything?) So, since arriv-
ing in the Los Angeles area where I've remained, except
for occasional lengthy forays abroad, I'd had my eye on Del
Mar. And not because it's an easy place to pick winners
either. No, picking winners is nice, but not really what
it's all about. What it's all about, in fact, is the the reason
for this book.

Actually, like most other horseplayers I know, I find
Del Mar a tough track to handicap. This is primarily be-

cause the season runs from late July to early September, just after the big race meetings at Santa Anita and Hollywood Park. The older, better-known horses have been running steadily and hard since late December and a lot of them have disappeared, at least temporarily, from the scene. Horses pour into Del Mar from all over, "pigs you ain't never heard of," as my friend Larry the Loser once put it, after a string of unfortunate selections. They come from the tracks around San Francisco, from the county fairs, and from Caliente, the dusty racing emporium across the Mexican border in Tijuana.

Also on the grounds are a lot of unraced two-year-olds who are being brought along slowly and carefully and about whom nobody knows much, even their trainers. Del Mar is not a place to wager with excessive confidence and I remember one dismal stretch a few years ago when I went to the window thirty-five times without picking a winner. But then one shouldn't go to Del Mar, or any racetrack, really, with the idea of making money. That isn't what makes the sport, or is it?

One of the things that Del Mar does evoke is the relaxed, easygoing feeling of what horse racing used to be before the advent of the tote board and the discovery by the politicians that there was money to be made from it. (The money men now cut a 15.75 percent slice of the California racing melon, which means that suckers like myself can expect to get back only about eighty-four cents out of every dollar we wager, and it's worse in New York. We are bucking a tiger, as they'd put it in Vegas.) A track employee once characterized Del Mar as a place "where nobody's in a hurry but the horses." It's small and intimate and sits in a pleasant valley flanked by rolling hills and the sea. A cool breeze usually blows off the water while the patrons stroll about the paddock area or sit in the shade of the stands and the horses perform out there on the dirt track or the bright-green infield turf course. The desperate, hunted look of too many of the patrons at the larger tracks is mostly missing here. About forty percent of Del Mar's fans come from the L.A. area, but they aren't the ones who'll show up just to gamble their grocery money or their welfare checks. The place is still just a little too far out of reach for that, so it becomes not too hard at Del Mar to imagine again a vanished era of casual sport and pure fun. "What this is, it's more of a mood, a way of life," old Oscar Otis, who used to write a daily column for the *Racing Form,* once told me. "It's racing, all right, but with this important difference—it's a great place to relax."

Nobody in the whole world, except possibly Perry Como, has ever been more relaxed than Bing Crosby, so it's entirely appropriate that he should have been the one to launch Del Mar, thirty-eight years ago. He was living in nearby Rancho Santa Fe when the people building facilities for a San Diego County Fair, which also included a mile racetrack on the premises, ran out of money. Crosby, an established student of Thoroughbred horse flesh, quickly organized the Del Mar Turf Club, holding his election for officers, appropriately enough, on the War-ner Brothers lot in Burbank, and signed a ten-year lease with the Fair people. The fact that they eventually had to lend their landlords the money to finish the facilities they had leased didn't phase them at all. Nothing ever ruffled Crosby, and in the likes of Pat O'Brien, his vice president, and such other associates as Oliver Hardy, Gary Cooper, Leo McCarey, and Joe E. Brown he had surrounded himself with an unflappable, well-heeled, and supremely glamorous array of plungers. By the time opening day came around, on July 3, 1937, a lot of the paint on the premises was still a little wet, but at least a roof had been put on the grandstand and the horses were ready to run.

About fifteen thousand people showed up that first day and Crosby and O'Brien were there to greet them in person. They went right down to the turnstiles to check in the first arrivals. Crosby, of course, was dressed in a floppy sports shirt and yachting cap, though later he donned a bright-blue jacket, white slacks, and a straw boater for the official opening ceremony in the infield. "We hope you all enjoy the meeting and have a measure of success at the payoff windows," he told the crowd in his fanciest informal style.

They were slow, however, getting the first race off. The special train that the Santa Fe Railroad had dispatched, loaded with hard knockers from L.A., was late. When it finally appeared through a gap in the hills just north of the track, everybody cheered. Cheering for the train, in fact, became a Del Mar tradition, whether it was late or not, and only died when the railroad discontinued the service in more recent times. Anyway, the first race did finally get off at 2:24 P.M. and a gelding named High Strike led all the way to win it. This could have made some people suspicious, since the animal happened to be owned by Mr. Crosby himself, but it didn't. Everybody reportedly cheered even louder than before. It was an auspicious beginning, and when eighteen thousand people showed up on the second day, betting nearly a quarter of a million dollars on their selections, everybody assumed that big-time racing had come to Del Mar to stay.

Attendance, however, tailed off pretty drastically after those first two days and Del Mar ultimately attracted an average of fewer than five thousand patrons a day. That hundred miles from L.A. was then, in Oscar Otis's words, "a tortuous journey." The trains were slow, the roads poor, the airlines nonexistent. The difficulty of the trip and the limited patronage Del Mar attracted at least saved its original relaxed, old-fashioned air. Like Saratoga, Del Mar survived through the years as a Mecca for those of us who like to think of horse racing as something a little better than a crap game or a numbers racket.

For the people running it, however, the main problem was to make the operation pay. Under the Crosby–O'Brien regime the tactic adopted was to turn out the celebrities, on the reasonable assumption that people would gawk first and bet later. During 1938, Crosby broadcast a half-hour radio show from Del Mar every Saturday afternoon. He'd stroll about the grounds interviewing the patrons, then retire to the premises of the Jockey Club where he'd belt out a couple of songs. Later, after the racing, large informal parties went on at the Jockey Club until the wee hours, with such entertainers on hand as Al Jolson, Danny Thomas, Tony Martin, the Ritz Brothers, Donald O'Connor, and Jimmy Durante, who always demolished his quota of pianos every season. Paramount even put on the world premiere of Crosby's latest movie, *Sing, You Sinners,* at the track. And then there was *the song,* probably the most famous racetrack ditty ever penned.

It was the wife of one of Crosby's writers who thought up the phrase "Where the Turf Meets the Surf," but Crosby himself and Johnny Burke collaborated on the rest of the lyrics, set to music by one James Monaco. Around Del Mar the chorus is as well-known as that of our national anthem: "Where the turf meets the surf/ Down at old Del Mar/ Take a plane, take a train, take a car/ There's a smile on every face/ And a winner in each race/ Where the turf meets the surf at Del Mar." As recorded by the master himself, this immortal ditty is still played before the first and after the last race of every program. "The only time I can stand that song," my friend Charlie the Barber once observed, "is if I've had at least four winners. On a losing day it's a dirge."

Crosby and his Hollywood pals gave up Del Mar in the late nineteen-forties and since then a series of managements has operated the track, not always remuneratively. San Diego is a sluggish, conservative navy town and surrounded by suburbs teeming with retired fatcats. Most of them are not horseplayers and the relatively few there are tend to prefer Caliente, where they race on weekends year-around and bettors can try to pick a six-horse parlay to hit a giant jackpot and also get bets down at tracks all over the country, including Del Mar. Until the completion of the freeway a few years ago finally cut the travel time from L.A. down to about two hours, racing at Del Mar remained a financially marginal operation. Today the place is run by the Del Mar Thoroughbred Club, a nonprofit outfit composed largely of professional horsemen and committed to spending millions of dollars in revenue for improvements. Donald Smith, a lawyer and lithographer, who has been around the track in one capacity or another since 1945, is in charge and he once explained what he thought his group was up to by saying, "We're going to try to run this place for fun's sake."

No racetrack today is operated purely for fun's sake anymore, as anybody knows who's spent any time recently at such racing supermarkets as New York's Aqueduct and Belmont, where the plants are huge and impersonal and the horses so far away from the public that it's easier for most people to follow the races on the closed-circuit TV monitors. Luckily, Del Mar has so far not spent much on "improvements" and consequently the original charm of the place remains. The architectural theme, adapted by San Diegans Sam Hamill and Herbert Jackson from the romantic era of the Spanish missions, features a tower and main clubhouse entrance modelled on the Mission San Jose in San Antonio, while the façade of the grandstand and some of the exhibit buildings recall various California missions and ranchos. From the seaward side, in fact, Del Mar looks like something William Randolph Hearst might have dreamed up had he been overwhelmed by a passion for Old Spain. "There *is* a certain charm to this place," Don Smith once said. "It's like going racing in a church."

Coming down from L.A. by car, you first see the track when the freeway tops a rise and swoops down toward the plain again. To the right, toward the ocean, the grandstand suddenly looms emptily over the dirt oval and the lush, still virgin grass of the infield, while, closer still, the long, serried rows of barns hem the course in, flanked by roads and parking lots. On that bright sunny July day, as I headed the car for the exit ramp, I could smell the presence of the horses; the soft, musky scent of over sixteen hundred living animals wafted through the open windows of my car by a brisk sea breeze. My heart sang and I whooped. The seven weeks of the meeting seemed pleasurably endless then and each of the forty-three days the horses would run held a promise of rapture.

I checked into my motel, a large, rambling, Spanish-style structure built around a swimming pool and flanked by tennis courts, unpacked, and went out to have a look around. The first person I bumped into in the corridor was Larry the Loser. Larry is in his mid-thirties, has a fixed income from an estate managed, luckily for him, by his older brother, and has never, as far as I know, had a winning meeting anywhere. We greeted each other warmly.

"You down for the season?"

"Yes," I said. "You?"

He shrugged. "I don't know. I never did too good down here. How'd you do at Hollywood?"

"Not bad," I confessed. "I won."

"A lot?"

"Not bad."

"I shoulda waited a week, ya know? I mean, coming down here. You know what happened to me last year opening day?"

"No. What?" I couldn't have stopped him from telling me anyway.

"I bet this lock in the first and he died. In the second my pig folded up in the stretch and run fourth. Then I bet some horse which don't run a step because it's trained by some woman and I shoulda known better. The *schmutz* horse win the fourth and I don't get on it. I lay off the fifth and my selection win it. In the sixth I sock it in on something I really like and I lose to some first-time starter which don't show any works. Naturally I had the last three, only I am tapped out by this time so I got no way to bet 'em. I'm telling ya this track is murder, sheer murder."

Larry has total recall about every track he's ever been at, but it wouldn't matter. They're all murder to him.

2

Post Time

"Hey, Pete," the old groom called out, as horse and rider passed the long row of stalls on their way back from a morning gallop, "hey, that was some nice gal I seen you with last night."

"Nice?" the rider said, clucking to his still charged-up mount but keeping a tight hold on the reins, "nice? Man, she move me up three lengths."

I got up early on opening day and spent most of the morning walking around the backside, which is what the horsemen call the stable area of any track. I knew it well and I knew many of the people who worked there, so it wasn't a new experience for me but one that has never failed to give me pleasure, because, as in the theatre, I'm always happiest backstage. I like especially the casual camaraderie that is its heartbeat, with the horses moving in the fresh, early air back and forth from the track where the workouts are in progress, or being administered to around the stalls, each racing stable with its different atmosphere and style and its floating population of small animals—chickens, cats, dogs, goats, sheep, even pigs, each a member in good standing of a self-supporting, circumscribed little world. The racing people are gypsies, moving endlessly from track to track, caravans in avid search of the pot of gold at the end of an impossible rainbow. Every day brings triumph, disappointment, sometimes anguish and disaster, too many emotions lived through in too short a time, but always renewed hope, because each day is a new beginning, a new concatenation of small and large possibilities. The backside is where the dreams are dreamed, born in the glorious symmetry of a thousand pounds of bone and muscle in concerted, rhythmic action; witnessed and testified to by the cold, knowledgeable eyes of silent watchers; measured and recorded in the merciless, all but inaudible ticking of stopwatches. The backside is a drama, with comedy relief and no end of audience involvement.

"What you doin' here, man?" the tiny Mexican said, coming around the corner of the barn with his rake and catching sight of the lean, angry-looking black in his dirty work clothes. "I thought you was gettin' out. I thought you was not goin' to come no more. What you doin' now? You catch on somewhere?"

"Shit, no," the black replied, spitting contemptuously, his head shaking from side to side, denying his enslavement. "I didn't come here to work. I came here to bet."

"You one lyin' son bitch," the Mexican said, grinning. "You ain't got no money to bet with."

"Shit," the black said, "I don't need this." He spat

again and walked away, turning his back, like so many others there, to unwelcome reality.

Later that morning, I sat up in the guinea stand and gazed down over the track. Below me, in the still hazy light, the horses moved. Some worked close to the inside rail, their riders hunched over their shoulders and along their necks, demanding from their charges a measure of effort, a small but crucial testing of their talent; or they galloped past in the middle of the track, the riders erect in the saddle or standing high in the stirrups above their mounts, the reins gripped tightly to keep them from wasting any of their speed when it was not wanted. The thudding of hooves in the soft earth supplied the beat of sound above which the voices of the riders called out contrapuntally to each other, in warning or in jest or in casual observation, the horses coughing and snorting, oblivious to anything around them but the irresistible impulse within them to run, the instinct and desire bred into the marrow of every racehorse, as intrinsic to his needs as the beating of his heart. The sight and feel of it have never failed to move me, sometimes to fill me with an exultation I can't quite account for, as if, perhaps, such a manifestation of power, grace, spirit, and beauty could only be divine.

When the horses had finished either working or galloping, they came walking and trotting back in the opposite direction, moving in bunches along the outer rail, the riders relaxed, at ease now, all effort and strain behind them. The horses were headed back to the barns to be cooled out, rubbed, bathed, walked, petted, and fed and finally tucked away again in their stalls for the day. None of the ones I had seen that morning would be asked to run

competitively, to test themselves definitively that afternoon. For most their turn would come, but not then, not
just yet.

Across from where I sat, the grandstand yawned emptily, like the jaws of some science-fiction monster waiting
patiently for its prey. A few cars and campers and small
trucks had already turned into the parking lots, but the
gates to the grounds themselves were still closed to the
public and we were still hours away from post time. But
I could taste the excitement of the moment at the back of
my throat, as if I, too, were a participant, one of the many
whose immediate future would begin to be tangibly
weighed and measured that very afternoon.

They've had great days here, not as many, of course, as
at the more venerable racing establishments back East,
but fine times just the same. It was here, for instance, on
August 12, 1938, that rugged old Seabiscuit, the reigning
handicap champion of the West, beat off a tough challen-
ger from the Argentine named Ligaroti, holding him off
by a head in a match race at a mile and one-eighth for a
winner-take-all purse of twenty-five thousand dollars, no
mean sum in those days. It was also here, on Labor Day
1956, that Johnny Longden brought Arrogate home in
front in the Del Mar Handicap for the second straight
year. It was the 4871st victory of Longden's career, breaking the record held at the time by Sir Gordon Richards of
England. And I was present in 1970 when Willie Shoemaker, also on Labor Day, booted home winner number
6033 to surpass Longden, who was on hand to congratulate
him. Traditions, charm, great events, thrilling races—and
let the winners keep coming in, please.

"Hey, Rudy, how'd he go?" somebody called out from behind me to the journeyman jock, Rudy Campas, just then riding past below on a thin, nervous horse he'd worked three-quarters of a mile only minutes before. "He looked funny with that choppy stride."

"It's not funny," Campas said. "What's funny?"

"What'd you catch him in?" the voice asked.

"One fourteen and two," somebody else said.

"I got a goat runs faster than that."

"Yeah, you got nothin' but goats. The ones that ain't pigs."

Nineteen thousand people showed up by post time at two o'clock, a new record for an opening day. Valet and preferred parking were full an hour before and the cars trying to maneuver their way into the lots were nosed up against each other in long lines that stretched back for several miles in all directions, jamming the freeway and the access roads. Del Mar had never been designed to handle such an influx, but the people who finally made it inside all seemed cheerful and relaxed, unaware of or indifferent to discomfort. They came streaming in alone or, more usually, in small groups, some of them young couples holding children by the hand. The air was festive and informal, like that of a large company picnic. I stood by the main clubhouse entrance for a while and watched them come. In that sea of pleasure seekers it wasn't very hard to pick out the hard knockers, more than a few of whom I knew, middle-aged men like myself, mostly, with *Racing Forms* stuffed into their pockets and large binoculars slung over their necks and shoulders and about them the wary, poker-faced look of pros grappling with a tough racket.

Before the first race, a meaningless mile gallop for cheap platers, I went around behind the receiving barn and watched the horses come in, led by their grooms, each entry in the race with its own little entourage of trainers, owners, stablehands, friends, and casual well-wishers. As the animals filed past, Fred Sneddon, a Scot who's been doing this for longer than he cares to remember, checked their shoes, because all horses have to run in prescribed, approved equipment, and just beyond him another track official named Mel Price grabbed each horse's upper lip and peeled it back long enough to make sure the numbers permanently tattooed there conformed to the ones listed beside the horse's name on his fact sheet. Before lip tattoos were adopted a generation or so ago, it was easier to slip a ringer into a race, steal a purse, and cash some pretty nice bets. "It's not infallible," Price explained, "because the numbers deteriorate with time. Some of the eights begin to look like threes, for instance. But it's pretty safe."

I knew what Price meant. "I had this unraced two-year-old one time who was an absolute bullet," I was told once in a taped interview by a trainer I'll call Corrigan. "He looked exactly like one of my other horses, a four-year-old who couldn't run a step. We were racing down in Caliente then, before lip tattoos became the rule, and one day I entered the four-year-old in a race he figured to lose by twenty lengths, but I had to run him somewhere. Well, it's twenty-five minutes before post time and I'm about to put a saddle on this bum when I realized this Mexican groom I'd just hired the day before had brought the two-year-old in by mistake. Of course I knew the difference, but I told the Mexican to finish saddling him and I ran up to the head man's office and I told him what had happened. He thought it over and then he said, 'I don't know what you're talking about.' I turned to go and as I hit the door the guy added, 'Don't bet more than five hundred on him.' So I got out of there and I found a friend of mine to run my money through the windows a little at a time so it wouldn't show up on the board right away and then I went back down to the paddock. The bum was twenty to one and he should have been fifty. All I had to worry about now was the jockey. He'd ridden the bum several times and he knew the horse was no good. I pulled him aside and I told him I was betting fifty dollars for him and he was to take a good hold and not win by more than five lengths. The boy thought I was crazy, but all I told him was the horse would run today. Well, just before they go off, the odds on him go down to eight, seven, six, then five to one and I figure the head man and his pals are getting down on him pretty good. Did he win? Jesus, he opened up about forty lengths at the half and he come in by ten, with the boy standing up and goddam near strangling him to death in the stretch. You couldn't do that today."

I recalled this story as I stood there, waiting for the meeting to get under way. I had decided I wasn't going to bet this first race, so I was in no hurry and I stayed there, chatting with Sneddon and Price. After a while, the horses came back, filing past me through the gap on their way out to the track. The jockeys looked unconcerned, at ease, sitting high up on their mounts and relaxed before the heavy work ahead. When the procession hit the main track to the sound of a bugler blowing the familiar call to the post and *the song* began to boom out over the loudspeakers. I went upstairs and stood in the grandstand over the finish line.

As the horses neared the starting gate, I looked at my program, then at the *Form,* which I had rolled up and thrust into my side pocket. I rather favored an honest old horse in the race named Montana Winds and he was going off at a good price, but I figured he had seen better days and I didn't like the look of the heavy bandages on his rear legs. I stuck my resolve not to bet. And, of course, Montana Winds won, paying $16.60 for every two-dollar ticket. I regretted my cowardice only briefly because I had a good day overall and you can't, or shouldn't, bet every race anyway. "You can beat a race, but you can't beat the races" is the way the old saw goes. But wisdom, at the track, is a sometime thing at best.

3

It Just Makes a Man Sick

The jockey had ridden for the old trainer many times before and he knew the old man's horses pretty well. Lately, however, he'd been running into a lot of bad luck with them. Especially those last two races, when he'd gotten caught behind a wall of horses on the far turn and wasn't able to get clear in time to make a move. The old trainer had said nothing to him after those races and now the two men stood side by side in the walking ring, waiting for the paddock judge to call "Riders up!" The jockey was puzzled. The old man had always had something to say about each one of his horses, but today he was silent, hands jammed into his overcoat pockets and staring glumly straight ahead. The jockey looked at the horse he was going to ride in this race and he knew he was a late runner, but not much else about him. He gazed up at the trainer. "Any instructions?" he asked, as the paddock judge got ready to make his call.

The old man spat and kept his eyes averted. "Sure," he said. "Take a good hold on this sucker and keep him somewhere off the speed in here, but not too far back. Don't get fanned on the turn, but keep him off the rail where the dirt won't bother him so much. Just let him settle down and run on his own courage the first part. Then, when you get to the three-eighths pole, fuck up like you always do."

Reavis was sitting in the track kitchen alone just before the eight o'clock break on the morning of the second day and I went over and joined him. I like the kitchen in the early morning. It's a warm and convivial place, a large room with plain wooden tables and plastic chairs where the horsemen can sit, have breakfast or lunch or just a cup of coffee, and entertain themselves by telling each other lies. Reavis didn't look eager for company that morning, but I knew him well enough to risk intruding on his privacy. "Hello, Willis," I said, "how are you?"

He looked stolidly at me over the rim of his coffee mug. "Sick, Bill, just sick to death," he said.

He didn't look it. He's a sturdily built, heavyset man with thick wavy hair and the canny, good-humored features of a successful card shark. He's in his early sixties but looks ten years younger and strong enough to throw people through walls.

"Got the flu?" I asked. There was a lot of it going around.

"No," he said, "I'm just so disgusted I don't know what to do."

"I thought your horse would win that race," I said. "In fact, I bet him myself."

"Why, godamighty," Reavis said, slamming his mug

down on the table, "we shoulda won easy! All the boy had to do was follow instructions! It just makes you sick to work so hard to get a horse ready and then the boy won't do what you tell him to! You saw what he did, didn't you?"

I had, indeed. In the fifth race on opening day, Reavis had entered a horse called Burgeon in a contest on the turf course at a distance of a mile and one-eighth. Under Frank Olivares, one of the better jockeys at the meet, Burgeon had come out of the gate last, had lagged way behind the leaders, then had made a tremendous move on the turn for home, had come very wide and finished second, beaten by a neck. He had been the favorite, at odds of two to one, and I was reasonably sure that both Reavis and the horse's owner, a sharpshooter named Dick Gregorian, had bet on him pretty heavily. Off his recent form, Burgeon should not have been the favorite in the race. He had run badly at Hollywood Park, because the turf course there is very hard and stings his feet, but he had been expected to do well at Del Mar, where the turf is deep and soft. He's a big horse and, with all that weight, he needs that kind of footing to do his best.

"This horse has got a world of talent," Reavis explained, "but he's a big old stud and lazy. I told the boy to shake him up when the gate opened, just enough to get him interested right away, lay him up there no worse than fourth or fifth, then really work on him in the drive. Hell, the way he rode him we had no chance. Even then we might have won, if he don't come so wide. And you know what the boy told me when he got off? 'If I'd known what this horse could do, I'd have won by six,' he says. Why it just makes a man sick!"

After coffee, as we walked back to his barn together, Reavis reminisced about some of the other riders who had screwed him up during his long career. The names were familiar to me and I was properly sympathetic. I knew all about what jockeys disregarding instructions could accomplish. In fact, it's quite possible I'd still be in racing today as an owner if a jockey named Raul Caballero hadn't moved too soon, instead of too late, with a horse of mine, but that's a story I'm reserving for later. It's linked in my memory to some other events in my life, not all of them painful, that were not uppermost in my mind on this particular morning. Mainly, I was enjoying Reavis's reminiscences, because, like many old horsemen, he has a salty way with an anecdote.

"I had an owner once who liked some rider real well," Reavis recounted. "Can't remember the boy's name now, it was so long ago, but the owner insisted and insisted I use him, so I put this boy up on one of our horses one day and the owner and I sat together in his box and watched the race. The man was sitting in back of me and all during the race, you see, he's hitting me with this rolled-up *Racing Form.* He's cheering every move the boy makes and hitting me with this rolled-up newspaper and at the head of the stretch we take the lead and the owner, he's cheering and shouting and hitting me with the *Form* and he's saying to me, 'You see? You see? I told you! I want that boy on *all* my horses!' Only, just at the wire there, this other horse come up and beat us a head. This owner don't stop shouting or hitting me with the *Form,* only now he's screaming at the rider. 'You dirty louse!' he shouts."

At Reavis's barn, we stopped in front of Burgeon's stall.

"That's Bur*goon* there," Reavis said. "Look at that sucker now. He was so mean when I got him last year you couldn't go near him. Now he's like a big dog."

"Bur*goon*?" I asked. "Is that how you pronounce it?"

Reavis ignored my question. He has his own way of pronouncing his horses' names and he's not about to be put off by some Eastern-educated smartass like me. Bur*goon* it is; it sounds better than Burgeon anyway. "What do you think of these riders here?" Reavis asked the horse. The animal snorted and raised his upper lip in a magnificent sneer. "He don't like the stewards none either," Reavis said, grabbing the horse's lip and pulling it affectionately. "Just like a big dog now."

"When are you planning to run him again?" I asked.

"There's another race in this series next week," he said. "I'll run him then. Olivares wants him back." I must have looked astonished, because Reavis added: "What am I going to do, Bill? If I change riders now, I'll get some boy who don't know this horse. At least Olivares won't make the same mistake next time. Bill, the way some of these boys ride out here, it just makes you sick to your stomach."

4

We Had the Horse Right There

"How'd you like to buy a piece of a good two-year-old?" the voice on the telephone asked. It belonged to a friend of mine named Duke Waxenberg and he was actually suggesting that I invest in a racehorse. It could have been worse; he could have been peddling me a bridge. I told him I was mad, but not quite as mad as all that and hung up on him.

I spent the next twenty minutes wandering around in a daze while a furious debate raged in my head, with the forces of reason doing most of the talking. Thoroughbreds are expensive and, even as yearlings, can cost a quarter of a million dollars or more. Most of the twenty thousand foals born every year never even get to the races and less than four percent of them ever win a stakes race. Horses start running professionally as two-year-olds and about seventy percent of all two-year-olds buck a shin at one time or another, a minor injury that nevertheless can knock a horse out of training for weeks. There are dozens of other ailments that afflict Thoroughbreds, some of them serious enough to immobilize them permanently, and none of them are rare. Worse, a horse may not run well simply because he doesn't feel like it. The stables are full of so-called morning glories who burn up the track in the morning and die in the afternoon. The trouble is, they don't really die; they go right on eating. It now costs between seven hundred and eight hundred dollars a month to keep one of them in active training at a major track and that's not including vet bills. In other words, the buying and racing of Thoroughbreds is an expensive and foolhardy pastime, not unlike playing the stock market on margin or investing in a Broadway play. Most of the time you lose.

So much for the forces of reason. The fact is I'd been caught with my resistance down. The year was 1967 and I had just sold a novel of mine to some swinish types at a movie studio. I had a sizeable chunk of money I was anxious to keep the IRS from savaging. I rationalized that I could always deduct my losses. Also, I'd been living in Los Angeles for a couple of years, after having spent most of my life in the East and in Europe, and the balmy L.A. life-style tends to soften your brains. Back in New York, no one could have sold me any part of a horse; out West, blinded by smog and baked silly by sunshine, anything seemed possible. I called Duke back. "I'm still not interested," I said, "but tell me more."

Five of us bought the horse. His name was War Flag and he was an unraced two-year-old colt, foaled in Kentucky at the Calumet Farm, a top racing establishment. His sire was My Babu, a celebrated English stakes winner, and the mare's daddy was Bull Lea, one of racing's super-studs. The colt's credentials were impeccable and, if he turned out to be a runner, we stood to make a fortune in stud fees after he was through racing. Best of all, his trainer, a man named Willis Reavis, said he was only weeks away from his debut. We paid a total of thirty-five thousand dollars, including taxes and a reserve to tide us over the first couple of months. I'm not sure which piece of him I bought, but I have my dark suspicions.

I never set eyes on War Flag until the day he ran his first race at Del Mar, a couple of weeks after we bought him, and I drove down for the occasion from Malibu, where I was then living. Certain vivid images from that day will always remain with me. The way War Flag looked, for instance, when he was led out into the bright sunshine of the paddock. (My God, I'd bought the most magnificent horse since Pegasus, a paragon of a beast with a dark, gleaming coat and the noble head of an Elgin Marble!) My partners and I stood around grinning stupidly while Reavis instructed our jockey, Dean Hall, hoisted him lightly into the saddle, and sent horse and rider on their way to glory. I remember the bright-yellow lights of the tote board winking the odds at us and the growing confidence I felt as War Flag, who had opened at twelve to one, clicked down until at post time he had been established by the bettors as the favorite, at two to one. I spent most of the next ten minutes at the windows making bets of my own on him, then got to our box and sat there for what seemed an eternity as the horses fidgeted in the starting gate. When they finally exploded into the clear, War Flag tucked in along the rail and dropped

back to fourth, until Hall took him out to find running
room at the head of the stretch.

Yes, War Flag won his first race. Acording to the chart
caller for the *Racing Form*, he "responded to light urging
on the stretch turn and won going away while well in
hand." It was only a six-furlong race for a twenty-five
hundred-dollar purse against untried competition, but it
could just as well have been the Kentucky Derby as far as
we were concerned. I must have been jumping up and
down because I popped two buttons on my jacket, my
wallet flew out of my inside pocket, and I smashed the
unbreakable crystal on my wristwatch. But so what? I
had the big horse wheeled in the daily double to everything in the second race, I had my share of the winner's
purse, and obviously it was only a matter of months before
I'd be right up there, rubbing haunches with Ogden
Phipps, Jock Whitney, and Alf Vanderbilt. I remember
somebody in our box saying that we ought to make our
reservations for Louisville right now, since hotel rooms get
scarce there around Derby time, which, after all, was only
nine months away. The words I'll never forget, though, are
the ones Dean Hall spoke when he shook hands with us
in the winner's circle after we'd all had our picture taken
grouped around our champion. "I just tapped him once
and that was it," he said. "You got a real nice colt there."

After we'd all spent a lot of happy minutes at the
cashiers' windows and reunited again in our box, Reavis
told us he'd race War Flag one more time during the meeting at Del Mar, probably two weeks later in a twenty-five-
thousand-dollar stakes race on the infield turf course. Our
winning share of that purse, we figured out, would be

about fourteen thousand dollars, which buys a lot of hay. After that, War Flag would take it easy for a few months until the winter racing at Santa Anita. "We'll be going for big purses there," Reavis explained. "And if he comes along the way it looks right now, we should do all right with him."

Doing all right was not exactly what any of us had in mind that day. We were an oddly assorted group, I realized. I was a writer. Al Rappaport was a physicist who also invented household gadgets and dabbled in oil. Howard Kosh was a stockbroker. Jerry Shanberg worked for an outfit that rented furniture and party favors. Duke Waxenberg was a Beverly Hills *boulevardier* and *bon vivant.* About the only thing we had in common was horse fever and the newly acquired conviction that we were all about to become very rich. What did Reavis mean by "doing all right"?

I then took my first really close look at the trainer. A typical horseman, I said to myself, and typical horsemen are tight-fisted gamblers who vote Republican. It's all right, Willis, I wanted to tell him, you just go back to the barn, take care of the horse, and play your Lawrence Welk records. Destiny calls, baby.

If destiny ever did call, the line must have been out of order. War Flag never did win another race for us and to this day I'm not sure why. To begin with, he did not run again at Del Mar. Something about the infield turf course being too hard for his tender feet, according to Reavis, or was it that he had bumped himself in his stall and come up lame for a couple of days? Anyway, better not take a

chance with our champion, the trainer said, with the much
more important and lucrative Santa Anita and Hollywood
Park meetings coming up.

What could we do but agree with the man? We sat it
out until Santa Anita opened on December 26. The wait
drained away the approximately fourteen hundred dollars
in purse money we had won at Del Mar, but never mind.
We never doubted we had a real good one in the barn
and maybe we were right. I went out a couple of times in
the early morning to watch War Flag work and he looked
every bit as impressive as he had at Del Mar. But something Reavis said to me in the track kitchen one day, after
War Flag had breezed five-eighths of a mile in good style,
has stuck with me. He began by observing that he was sure
War Flag would improve as the distances of his races got
longer, then added, "But you can't never tell. I been around
this business all my life and the only good horses I ever
had was geldings. You don't know what these studs are
gonna do, especially when the mares come into season. Just
getting them to eat is a problem. Well, maybe we'll be
lucky."

We weren't. On December 29, War Flag, with Dean Hall
up, came out on the track for the seventh race as the seven
to one third choice of the bettors. He broke well, then
dropped steadily back and finished a dismal eighth in a
field of eleven. We sat in our box, paralyzed by the disaster. Howard Kosh looked as if his favorite stock had just
dropped twenty points. Reavis, who had gone down to talk
to the jockey, never did come back and it wasn't until the
next day that we found out what had happened.

War Flag, it seems, had popped a curb, which is a small

bone about the size of a man's thumb just under the hock. It was seven weeks before he ran again. This time he broke last, threw his head to one side and swerved when Hall tried to make up ground by coming through on the inside at the turn. He finished ninth in a field of ten. A week later, with a new and stronger-armed jockey named Bill Harmatz in the saddle, War Flag ran about an eighth of a mile, then bolted for the outer rail as the other horses swept past him. Harmatz was forced to pull up or risk ending in the parking lot. "Mean, mean," Reavis muttered, "he's so mean now he don't even want to be near other horses."

After that performance, the Santa Anita stewards barred War Flag from racing until he could prove in training that he wouldn't be a menace to himself and to everybody else. Reavis suggested that we geld him. "He just don't like other horses," he said. "He wants no part of them and tries to get out when the gate opens. He's a stud, all right." The trouble was the five owners couldn't agree what to do. Jerry was with Reavis, Duke disagreed and Al, Howard, and I were undecided. "If we geld him, we've got nothing after his racing days are over," said Duke. "You've got nothing anyway, if he doesn't win," said Jerry. "Thirty-five thousand dollars' worth of nothing," said Howard.

We decided to try some less drastic measures first. Reavis sprinkled saltpeter or something equally calming in War Flag's feed bin. Blinkers were added. A stronger bit was substituted. A specialist in handling fractious beasts coached War Flag in trials out of the gate. Nothing worked. After a couple of weeks the stewards reinstated our animal, but in races he simply wouldn't run. "All right, all right, do it!" Duke snapped one afternoon, just after Howard had observed sweetly that War Flag had just lost by only twenty lengths rather than the thirty we had become accustomed to.

War Flag's testicles were removed early one morning and Reavis was full of wonder at the event. "They was just as big as coconuts," he announced. "How he could run with them things back there I just don't know. Must have hurt something terrible."

He couldn't run too well without them things back there either, we discovered when War Flag came back out on the track a couple of months later at Hollywood Park. Nor was it any consolation at all that he was now losing races by only ten and twelve lengths. "We cut him too late," opined Reavis gloomily. "He don't even know he ain't got them balls no more."

"How can we get the message across to him?" Duke asked. "Singing telegrams?"

"Isn't it just possible that we bought an overrated horse?" I said to Jerry one day. "I mean, his winning time at Del Mar wasn't that fast, if you want to be cold-blooded about it."

We got very cold-blooded about War Flag. After all, he was draining hundreds of dollars out of our pockets every month. We began entering him in claiming races, which is a way of putting a selling price on your horse, and, as he continued to lose, we dropped the price on him from race to race. And the inevitable happened. War Flag appeared one afternoon with a price tag of sixty-five hundred dollars on him and somebody grabbed him. Interestingly enough, he ran his second-best race for us that day, making one real move at the leaders before once again drop-

ping out of it. I watched him being led away after the race
by his new owners, the red claiming tag dangling from his
halter, with relief but also a good deal of regret and a
nagging feeling that somehow we had let him down, all of
us, including Reavis.

I think now that my nagging feeling was correct. Over
the next two years, War Flag, running in similar company
and for a variety of different owners, won about thirty
thousand dollars in purses. He ran far too often to stay
sound and never did achieve anything but mediocrity. He
became what is known in racing parlance as a useful horse,
an animal that pays his way and a little bit more. The last
time I saw him was at the L.A. County Fair grounds in
Pomona, where he competed against real cheapies around
the tight turns of the bull ring, as these half-mile tracks
are known. By that time he had a knee that looked like a
cantaloupe. I bet on him that day and he won, but I never
heard of him again. I feel badly about him and what we
did to him. He may not have been a great horse, but he
was my first one and he paid for our overblown expecta-
tions and mistakes.

5

A Mortal Lock

Charlie looked absolutely frantic. He was standing by the paddock, half an hour before post time on the fourth day, looking for someone, anyone he knew. I was headed for the press box elevator and hoping to sneak past him unnoticed, but he saw me, rushed over through the incoming crowd, and grabbed my arm. "Are you holding?" he asked.

"Charlie," I said, "the first race hasn't even gone off. How can you be busted already?"

"Were you here for the ninth yesterday?"

I nodded.

"Then you know."

"Know what, Charlie?"

"The three horse in that race was a mortal lock," Charlie explained, "only he was one to two, so I took some Exactas off him to the one, the seven, and the eight. That six horse, the one that came in second, doesn't belong in there, so I didn't use him. It killed me. I need a couple of hundred."

"Charlie—"

"Yeah, yeah, I know you don't lend money at the track," he continued, cutting me off, "but listen." He went on to explain that succor was on its way, in the person of an old friend driving down with fresh money from L.A., but the friend had started late and might not make it by the fifth, another Exacta race in which Charlie had a mortal lock. The Exacta is a form of wagering requiring the bettor to pick two horses to finish first and second, in that order; you can buy any number of tickets, of course, on different pairings and the payoffs can be high, but essentially, like all combination wagers and parlays, it's a sucker bet. It's hard enough to pick one horse to do something right in a race, let alone two or more. Charlie knows this as well as I do, but it never stops him from trying. He must have been desperate to ask me for money, because I've always turned him down in the past. It's not that I don't trust him, especially, but I now have one inflexible rule at the track (or anywhere I'm gambling) and that is never to lend or to borrow money. It's not virtue on my part; merely self-defense.

Charlie Barber is an old racetrack chum of mine who claims he's a scriptwriter. He's about forty, tall, thin, and, when the betting frenzy is on him, as jittery as a heroin addict waiting for his fix. As far as I can tell, he's been working on the same script for eight years, an adaptation he made of one of Tennessee Williams's lesser efforts. We discuss this script two or three times a year, perhaps only so Charlie can revalidate his credentials in the real world, not for my benefit surely (because I don't care) but for himself. Charlie is hooked worse than most of us; he cannot stay away from the track even for a day. I have seen him bet hundreds on a single race and I can't imagine what his source of income is, but then this is true of a great many people I know at the track. They may drive old cars and have holes in their shoes, but they bet money by the fistfuls and always eventually seem to come up solvent again, no matter what disasters may befall them. It's one of the great mysteries of gambling in general that almost everybody manages somehow to stay in action most of the time. When I have a bad losing day, meaning that I may have lost as much as a hundred dollars, I've been known to take to my bed and stare at the ceiling for hours. I watch a movie up there in which my whole life passes before me as a series of cosmic blunders. To Charlie and his cronies, a hundred bucks barely gets them to their seats; they don't even know where the two-dollar windows are.

"Charlie, I'm sorry," I said. "I don't have two hundred. It has nothing to do with you, you know that."

"Yeah, yeah," Charlie said, his eyes now darting glances beyond me to the crowd moving past us. "It's OK, I'll get it."

"Who's your mortal lock?" I asked.

"The seven horse in the fifth. Cannot lose."

I looked at my program. The seven horse, Macadamian, a talented five-year-old sprinter with bad legs, figured to win, but he'd be a heavy favorite and was exactly the kind of horse I could never bet, primarily because he might break down anytime and the low possible return on money wagered did not justify the risk. Besides, I didn't believe

in the "mortal lock" anymore. The last mortal lock I bet
heavily on was Kelso, the greatest racehorse I've ever seen,
in a handicap in New York years ago. I drove in from my
summer cottage on Long Island just to bet him and I put
four hundred dollars on his nose at odds of less than even
money. When the gate opened, Kelso fell to his knees and
eventually finished fourth. It was only one of dozens of
ways he could have lost, of course, I realized later, but I
was a lot more naive then and still believed that the best
horse almost always wins the race. Kelso cured me of that
illusion, at least. "Charlie," I began, "the price'll be so
low—"

"He'll be better than even money," he said. "Everybody
knows he's unsound and hurting, but this horse just has too
much class for these others in here. He'll win on class
alone."

"Well, I hope you're right, for your sake."

But Charlie didn't even hear me; he'd spotted a possible
source of financing and rushed off to tap it.

The press box at Del Mar sits on top of the grandstand
roof directly above the stretch and the finish line and has
a wonderful view over the whole track. It is occupied daily
not only by the boys from the media and the *Form*, but
also, in separate cubicles of their own, by Harry Henson,
who calls the races for the public, and the three members
of the Board of Stewards, whose decisions govern the fortunes of everyone at the races, from the richest owner to
the lowliest two-dollar show bettor. Behind this long, low
rectangular shed row of offices is a small patio area with
tables and beach umbrellas and a snack stand presided

over by an ex-NHL hockey player named Dalton Smith, better known to all as Smitty. He's a small, tight-lipped man with iron-gray hair and a large nose who dispenses free sandwiches, soup, hotdogs, soft drinks, ice cream, and bad tips between his own trips to the two betting windows directly behind his emporium. The press box is the best place to watch the races, because at that height you can see exactly what happens on the turns, where horses get into the most trouble, and is the worst place to pick winners, because everybody up there dispenses inaccurate information. Almost everyone bets at the track, though employees are not supposed to, and I suspect even the stewards, those *chevaliers* supposedly *sans peur et sans reproche*, sneak a little money into the tote. Experts all and, like most experts, blinded by their own expertise.

The experts usually pick favorites and betting favorites in every race is the most direct route to poverty I know. Still, I couldn't find anyone in the press box this particular day who thought Macadamian could be beaten. Public confidence was cresting, too, on the strength of favorites winning three of the first four races and I felt sure that, with a trend so clearly established and all the plungers holding, Macadamian would go off at less than even money, an eventuality that would depress Charlie Barber but surely not deter him. After the fourth, I decided to go back downstairs and find out what Charlie was going to do and if he'd found a source of capital.

On my way to the elevator, I bumped into Barry Irwin, who is, I believe, the smartest and most reliable source of backside information, though no brighter than most of us in the use he makes of it at the betting windows. Barry wrote a daily column for the *Racing Form* and was usually

to be found in the early mornings in the stable area, listening, asking questions, and quietly trying to sift gleams of
reliable information for his column from the miasma of
tergiversation, exaggeration, and outright lying that characterizes backside gossip. Barry has been known to back
what he learns and believes to be true with sizeable chunks
of money, occasionally with disastrous results. Today, however, he was obviously connecting. Barry is in his early
thirties and has the face of a sixteen-year-old Jewish pixie,
but he can look sixty when his horses fail to perform as
expected and how he moves reflects the state of his fortunes. On good days, Barry bounces when he walks and
his boyish features acquire a near-rapturous look of self-
satisfaction. Today he was definitely bouncing. I asked him
how he felt about Macadamian.

"I hear he's so sore they couldn't even take him out of
his stall the other day," he informed me.

"Not a good bet, then, would you say?"

"He runs sore," Barry said. "He'll probably win."

"He'll be odds-on."

"If I liked him, I'd take him at one to ten."

"In a cheap Exacta race?"

Barry knew exactly what I meant. There are some races
it is riskier to bet on than others, especially when they feature heavy favorites running for small purses and belonging to owners and trainers who don't have many good
horses. Jockeys receive only thirty-five dollars to ride in a
race or ten percent of the winning purse. If the purse is
small, the riders can often make much more, especially in
Exacta and other combination-bet races, by letting the
longshots come in. (Riders aren't supposed to bet either,

but there's no way to keep them from doing so.) It's not that these races are fixed, in the sense that everyone knows beforehand exactly who will win, but it is a fact that the favorites in such races will often run very poorly, for reasons not apparent to the naked eye. Generally speaking, the beauty of money won betting at the track is that it can easily be hidden from the tax man. As I was writing this book, a jury in Maryland was finding four well-known jockeys at a racecourse guilty of conspiring to fix a Trifecta race and also of not declaring over thirty-five thousand dollars in winnings to the IRS. Obviously, somebody was inadequately paid off, because this sort of thing is almost impossible to police, though it happens all the time. What occasionally comes to light is the tiny tip of a very large iceberg.

Don Pierce, the jockey on Macadamian, is a supremely talented rider, one of the best in the business, but not one of my favorites. He has a funny habit of failing to get some of his horses out of the gate on time, which may, of course, be just bad luck but seems to happen to him a little too frequently. I had seen him do it, in fact, just two days earlier, on a two-year-old maiden filly breaking from the inside post at odds of six to five. Pierce had then rushed her up, but finished a well-beaten fourth. He took a lot of money down with him and led my friend Larry, who had bet on him, to observe that Pierce's photograph ought to be used to adorn post office walls. Another friend of mine once dubbed him "The Undertaker," a nickname that has stuck. I found myself wondering what Barry would make of all this and I told him.

"I'm not going to bet the race," he said, "but I sure

wouldn't let that kind of thinking discourage me, if I really liked the horse. That's pure bettors' paranoia."

I glanced over Barry's shoulder at the tote board just as the odds changed for the first time. Macadamian had been listed at nine to five in the morning line, the track's own estimate of what the odds would be, but went to one to five on the first flash, which reflected what the bettors themselves were actually doing. "Good God," Barry said, "and the horse can't even walk!"

Perhaps Macadamian couldn't walk, but he proved he could still run. He finally went off at odds of three to five and won easily, paying a straight $3.20 to win. A longshot named Hotshot's Profit ran second and the Exacta paid $79 for every five-dollar ticket, an excellent price, all things considered. I had missed Charlie before the race and I now hurried downstairs again to find out if he'd cashed a big bet on him.

Charlie was almost the first person I saw when I stepped out of the elevator at the second floor and walked into the grandstand area. He was leaning against the wall by an exit ramp and looked too sick to move. "Don't tell me your friend didn't make it in time," I said.

"He made it, all right," Charlie mumbled, "only I didn't bet the horse."

"Charlie, you're kidding! What do you mean you didn't bet him?"

He explained. His friend had arrived with the fresh money just before the fourth and Charlie had told him about Macadamian. The friend had gone off and, unknown to Charlie, bet a thousand dollars on the horse to win, just before the first flash of the odds. Charlie, then making his own leisurely way to the window, had seen the sudden dip to one to five and had been scared off. "I'd have bet him at even money," he said, "but at odds-on, sore as he is, he was no bargain. I couldn't play him."

"Not even in the Exacta?"

Charlie shook his head miserably. "I did play him in the Exacta, to three other horses but not that one."

"Charlie, you know what you've done?" I said. "You gave the horse to somebody else and it was his money that scared you off him. You realize that?"

"Tell me about it," Charlie moaned. "Go on and tell me about it. He made six hundred dollars on my information and I'm tap city again. Go on and tell me about it."

There are lots of ways to lose at the races, even on a mortal lock.

6

The Easy Way

This madness all began when I was sixteen years old and home from prep school on vacation. I was spending a weekend at my father's apartment in New York and that Friday night my beautiful cousin Isolde and her husband Harry came to dinner. I had never met Harry. All I knew about him was that he had money, that they lived in Washington, D.C., and travelled a good deal. However, I liked him right away. He was a tall, ingratiating man in his early forties with bright, deep-set eyes, curly hair, and an amiable smile. He was considerably older than Isolde, who was still in her twenties, but he seemed much younger than his years, perhaps because he didn't make the mistake of talking down to me. In the soft, upper-class drawl of his native Virginia, he regaled me with cheerful anecdotes about great sporting events and it soon became evident that he'd attended every major boxing match since the Dempsey–Firpo fight. When I discovered that he also possessed an encyclopedic knowledge of baseball, I was completely won over.

After dinner, on our way out of the dining room, Harry put his arm affectionately around my shoulders. "I'm certainly glad we had a chance to talk at last," he said. "We obviously share many of the same interests."

I asked him how long he and Isolde would be in town.

"Oh, just a few days," he said. "The card at Aqueduct looked so good this week it gave us an excuse to get to New York."

"The card?" I asked, puzzled.

"Harry goes to the horse races," my father said, with obvious sarcasm.

"The sport of kings," Harry said.

"Do you go, too?" I asked Isolde.

"Oh, no," she said, laughing. "I come to New York to shop."

The rest of the evening Harry talked about horses. He'd been enthusiastic about most sports, but I soon gathered that horse racing was his life. He had attended meets at every major track all over the world and he could apparently remember the name of every horse in every race he'd ever seen. He was full of long, detailed stories about the great races in which he'd won huge sums of money, usually by the length of a nose or an outstretched lip. And he relived each tense moment, often bounding to his feet at the climax of a story to give an exact imitation of the way a jockey whipped his tiring steed down the stretch or to recreate the eccentric running motion of some favorite front-runner. His ecstatic involvement was contagious and I listened, absorbed.

"You must have won a lot of money over the years," I said after a while.

"Harry doesn't talk much about the races he loses," my father observed drily.

Harry laughed. "Your father's right," he said. "It's not much fun when you lose."

"I've never seen a horse race," I said.

"I'm going out to Aqueduct tomorrow," Harry said. "Why don't you come along?"

I could immediately sense my father's disapproval, but I decided to ignore it and I told Harry I'd be delighted. My father wasn't exactly a spoilsport, but he used to write me letters full of good advice. "So far as business is concerned," he said in one of them, "we know that only hard work will ever produce results," and occasionally he'd remind me that at twenty-one I'd be entirely on my own and I'd better begin to think about a profession.

The trouble was that I had this secret conviction that the making of money was basically a frivolity, one of those harmless pastimes, like butterfly collecting and croquet, that no grown-up could take seriously. The way Harry talked, you could make thousands betting on horses and it fitted in with how I felt about money in general. I didn't underrate its importance, but I wasn't about to devote my life to it. Here was my father, a classical scholar and musician, wasting his time as a talent agent. That wasn't for me and I had already told him so, which had inevitably led to a certain amount of friction between us. I now told him that I could see nothing wrong with betting on horses, which struck me as reasonably sane compared to such other gambling propositions as the stock market, and I intended to look into it.

Harry chuckled, but my father only looked at him grimly. "If you have one of your usual days," he said, "it will be a good lesson for him."

At noon the next day, Harry and I met in a bar on the Long Island level of Penn Station. He was more sportily dressed than the night before, in a plaid sports jacket, gray slacks and an ascot, but his entire demeanor had changed. Though he greeted me cordially enough and ordered me a tomato juice, he was too engrossed in his newspaper to pay any further attention to me. From time to time he'd stop peering intently at the page he was reading just long enough to scribble some hasty notations on the margin. I maintained a discreet silence and sipped my tomato juice. Finally, after about twenty minutes of this, Harry suddenly glanced at the wall clock and stood up. "Come on, boy," he said tersely. "I don't care about the first race, but I've got to get something down on Velvet Glove in the second." He tucked the paper under his arm, picked up a black doctor's satchel from under the table, and swept us out at a gallop into the station. We bounded down a flight of stairs and entered a waiting railroad car just as the doors started to close.

The car, an antiquated Long Island model with parallel rows of cracked-leather seats, seemed to be full of small, round men smoking cigars and also reading newspapers. All the seats were taken and standees were packed in a dense, sweating mass up the aisle. We remained standing on the platform and, as the train began to move slowly out of the station, Harry put the satchel down between his feet and resumed his intense scrutiny of the newspaper. It wasn't until we were well out of the tunnel and curving down past Jamaica that Harry again took notice of me. With a deep, contented sigh he folded up the paper, stuffed it into his side pocket and lit a cigarette. "That gives me a pretty good start," he said and glanced out the window. "Well, I see we're almost there."

"What kind of paper was that you were reading?" I asked.

"Oh, I should have told you," he said. "That's the *Daily Racing Form*. It has all the past and present data on the horses running in each race at all the tracks. You can't really handicap a race without it."

"Could I see it?"

"Certainly," he said and handed me the paper.

The first two or three pages were concerned with news stories on various sporting events, but most of the paper consisted entirely of the names of horses, each one appearing over a large block of complex, indecipherable information consisting mostly of numbers and abbreviated names, words, and phrases. None of it made any sense to me, but finally, in a section devoted to the doings at Aqueduct that afternoon, I came across the name Velvet Glove. "Is this the one you're betting on?" I asked.

Harry nodded and glanced nervously around at the other passengers. "Yes," he said in a low voice. "He hasn't done much and he ought to go off at six to one or better."

"If he hasn't done much, what makes you think he can win?"

Harry jabbed a forefinger at the meaningless block of information. "Look here," he said. "See that? He breaks fast. In every race he's ever run he gets out in front."

"I gather he doesn't stay there," I said.

"That's just it," Harry said. "Those races were all at a mile or more and he was carrying a lot of weight. Today he's in with cheap horses at only six furlongs and he's not giving weight away to anyone. If he breaks on top, he could do it. And the price will be lovely."

"How do you know all that about him?" I asked. "Is it all in here?"

"Let me show you something," Harry said and held the paper out between us. "See these lines here?"

"Yes. What about them?"

"That's what the horse has done in all of his most recent races."

"You mean all you have to do to figure out the winner is learn how to interpret this gibberish?" I asked.

Harry smiled. "Well, not quite," he said calmly, with what I now realize was incredible patience. "There are unknown factors."

"Like what?"

"Sometimes a horse simply won't run," he explained, "no matter what the figures say."

I peered more closely at the exotic hieroglyphics on the page before me and I'd have asked more questions, but the train slowed down and the passengers began to mass toward the doors. Harry thrust the *Racing Form* back into his pocket and picked up his black satchel. I noticed that he was sweating slightly and that his eyes had a strange abstracted look. As the train came to a halt, he put a hand on my shoulder and pushed me toward the exit. "We only have a few minutes before post time," he said tersely. "If we get separated, we'll meet at the bar on the main floor of the grandstand, near the finish line."

The rest of that memorable afternoon flashed past with dizzying speed, leaving me only a jumble of sharp impressions. I member that, in the surge past the entrance to the racetrack, Harry and I did become separated, but not before he'd thrust a ten-dollar bill into my hand and said, "Velvet Glove is number four. Bet to win!"

A few minutes later I found myself standing indoors under a large electric board featuring all sorts of different numerals, while, over a loudspeaker, a harsh voice announced that the horses were nearing the starting gate. "Where do I make a bet?" I asked a man next to me and was rewarded with a look of amazement.

Eventually somebody came to my rescue and I joined a long line of people shuffling slowly toward a small window behind which a man in shirtsleeves was taking money and punching a ticket machine. I had no sooner paid my ten dollars and received my slip of cardboard in return than a bell sounded and I heard a roar from the crowd outside. People began running away from the windows and up the ramps leading, I gathered, to the track itself. I joined them and fought my way out into the open just as a knot of horses flashed past below me and three people directly in front of me began jumping up and down and pounding each other on the back. Beside me a huge black man under a light-blue derby slowly tore a wad of tickets into shreds and began to curse loudly. "What happened?" I asked him.

"What happened?" he shouted. "The fuckin' race was fixed, that's what happened!"

I went back inside and found Harry at the bar. His ascot had come undone and he was sweating heavily. The *Racing Form,* now beginning to look slightly soiled, was sticking out of his pocket, the black satchel was tucked under his arm, and his expression was ecstatic. "How about that?" he said, as soon as he saw me. "How about that? He paid better than five to one!"

"You mean Velvet Glove won the race?" I asked.

"My God, don't you know?" he barked happily. "Stayed in front all the way like I said he would!"

It was only the beginning. Harry's first five choices came in, all but one of them at odds of three to one or better. We spent most of our time standing in line—Harry at the hundred-dollar window, I at the ten-dollar one—either waiting to collect our winnings or to bet on the next race. After each triumph we'd meet again at the bar to embrace each other and toast our success.

After a horse named Apache won the sixth race by a nose and Harry came back from his window holding great wads of money in his fist, a crowd of watchful admirers began to gather around us. Harry quickly stuffed the money into his pants pocket and patted the black satchel. "I'm sure glad I brought this," he said.

"What's in there, anyway?" I asked.

Harry opened the satchel and shoved it under my nose. It was full of losing parimutuel tickets from all over and dating back several months. "They've got an Internal Revenue man sitting by the big-money windows," he said.

"When I went back this time to collect, he asked for my name and address and I just shoved the open bag under his face. I can prove I lost thirty thousand dollars last year alone."

"Say, Mister," one of our fans piped up, "what do you like in the next race?"

Harry took out his *Form* and glanced over the entries as the watchers pressed in around us. He finally shook his head and handed me the paper. "Maiden fillies," he said. "There's no sense even trying to handicap it." He winked at me. "You pick it, Billy."

"Me? I don't know anything about it."

"Just pick one, for the hell of it."

My first selection ever, an unsung filly named Que Hora, won by a neck and paid off at nineteen to one. Back at the the bar, Harry was whooping and hollering and buying everyone rounds of drinks. "Good Lord," was all he said, "we could just throw the damn *Form* away!"

Slightly dazed, I began to count my money. It amounted to several hundred dollars and seemed a vast fortune to me at the time.

"Well, how do you feel?" Harry asked as I finished counting my loot.

"Fantastic," I said. "Is it always like this?"

"Not always," Harry said. "I'll explain it to you later."

We left the track in a pink haze of glory without betting the last race of the day, because, as Harry put it, it was strictly for plugs and we shouldn't insult our luck. Our departure caused dismay in the ranks of our admirers, several of whom followed us as far as the exit gate in a vain attempt to persuade us to tell them who was going to win that last one.

As we rode back to town in a rented limousine, Harry explained the facts of life to me. "Not every day can be like this one," he began and went on to say that, over the year, he usually lost far more than he won. "If you bet every race," he concluded, "you can't help but lose. To me it doesn't matter because I can afford it and I like the excitement."

"You mean we were just lucky?" I asked. "There isn't any sure way of winning?"

It was then that Harry told me about Pittsburgh Phil, a gambler who had flourished in Chicago some years before. According to Harry, Pittsburgh Phil had made a fortune betting on horses. His system was to wait for a race in which his selection was almost certain to finish third or better, and then bet a large amount on his choice to show. "Betting to show usually pays less than even money," Harry said, "but it's safer. Of course you have to wait for the right race, sometimes for days, and you have to have some capital to make the bet worthwhile." He sighed and leaned back in his seat. "I could never do that," he said. "It's too boring."

That night we stopped first at their hotel to pick up Isolde, who had spent the day moving like a Mongol horde through the Fifth Avenue luxury department stores; then we had dinner at "21," paid fifty dollars apiece for tickets to *Oklahoma*, and sat at a ringside table for the last show at the Copacabana. When I finally got back to my father's place, I found him still awake. He was propped up in bed reading something light by Thucydides, in the original Greek.

"How did it go?" he asked.

"Oh, Harry made about fourteen G's and I took away a few hundred," I said casually.

My father shut his book with a decisive little slap. "Of course you know that Harry loses a lot more than he wins," he said.

I yawned. "That's because he doesn't care. Pittsburgh Phil played safe and made millions."

My father stared at me. "Jesus Christ!" was all he said.

A couple of days later I went back to school and several years passed before I finally had a chance to test Pittsburgh Phil's infallible system. I was always away, either at school or in the country, and my graduation was followed by fifteen inglorious months in the service. But it wouldn't have made any difference where I was, because I didn't have the capital to give the system an honest tryout. While still at school I contented myself by subscribing to one of the racing journals and making a careful study of its intricacies. I also read books on the subject and for a long time I kept a notebook in which I recorded the outcome of all my imaginary bets at New York racetracks. Once, when my father wrote me another of his Horatio Alger letters, I sent him back a sheet of paper with a complete account of my most recent hypothetical winnings and a brief accompanying note in which I informed him that his theories about dedication to a chosen task were obviously outmoded; no one in his right mind would work hard to make money if it could be made easily.

Finally, in the fall of 1945, I was discharged from the service and found myself in New York with no prospects, no ambitions, and several hundred dollars in separation pay in my pockets. My family wanted me to go back to college, but I wanted to study for the opera (I had a good lyric tenor voice) and find some way to support myself while doing so, since my father was utterly opposed to my going into any form of show business. My capital amounted to about five hundred dollars, not nearly enough, but I intended to be conservative and content myself, at first, with a modest income. What Pittsburgh Phil had done with tens of thousands, I would do with a few hundred.

My father was outraged. "Don't tell me you haven't outgrown that imbecile idea," he said.

"You like to do things the hard way," I answered. "I like to do them the easy way."

The next day I went out to the track, waited all afternoon in the rain to make one cautious bet and came home with a twelve-dollar profit. Both my fond parents were unimpressed, but I was filled with quiet elation. I went out faithfully every day after that, continued to play Pittsburgh Phil's system and invariably won. My earnings were meager (never more than eighty dollars a week and usually nearer fifty), but I consoled myself by thinking with glee of my friends, all of whom were either back in school or working at mundane jobs. I was absolutely convinced that I had solved the money problem and that I'd soon be earning enough to live, if not like a king, at least like a prince. It didn't bother me at first that I had no time to work on my voice, because that would come a bit later, when I could up the ante at the track a bit.

I had been doing things the easy way for about two months when I came home one night and went to bed with a high fever. My father sent his doctor over the next day and was told that I had nothing more than a very bad cold. "He's run-down," the doctor said. "Maybe he's been working too hard."

"Working too hard?" my father snapped. "All he does is go to the track."

"Well, whatever he's been up to," the doctor said, "it doesn't agree with him."

During the week it took me to recuperate I had a lot of time to think over this curious diagnosis and I began to wonder about Pittsburgh Phil and the life of ease. On a piece of paper I drew up a schedule of a typical day among the loafers:

10 A.M.–11 A.M.	Get up, instant coffee, scan paper for late scratches, leave house.
11 A.M.–11:30 A.M.	Subway ride to Penn Station, standing on crowded platform.
11:30 A.M.–12:30 P.M.	Train ride to track, reading *Form* and standing on crowded platform.
12:30 P.M.–1 P.M.	Enter track, check odds, eat lunch standing at crowded counter.
1:15 P.M.–5:45 P.M.	Watch races while keeping track of odds, checking *Form*, standing in ticket lines.
5:45 P.M.–6:45 P.M.	Train ride back to city, standing on crowded platform.

6:45 P.M.–7:15 P.M.	Subway ride home, standing on crowded platform.
7:15 P.M.–10:30 P.M.	Dinner break.
10:30 P.M.–2:30 A.M.	Buy next day's *Form*, handicap all races, soak feet.

When I added up all my figures, I discovered that, for an average net profit (before taxes) of $52.37, I had been working a six-day, seventy-two-hour week. Furthermore, I was excluded from all welfare benefits such as Social Security, pension plans, profit-sharing, and health insurance. Worst of all, I wasn't having any fun. I lay in bed and stared into my future—a succession of bleak and hopeless days, an infinity of servitude and unrewarded toil. I came to the conclusion that Pittsburgh Phil must have had the constitution of an iron ox and the dogged determination of Sisyphus.

I said nothing to either of my parents, but, on my first day out of bed, I went out and got a job. Eventually, my mother gave me enough money to go to Italy to study and I never again went to the races with the idea of making a living there.

For a long time I never knew what had become of Harry. He and Isolde got divorced and I lost track of him. A few years ago, however, I spotted him in the Turf Club during the Santa Anita meeting. He had put on weight and aged, of course, but otherwise looked much the same and I recognized him immediately. He was sitting alone at a table covered with small mounds of losing tickets and was intently scanning the *Form*. I went over and said hello, but had to remind him who I was. "My goodness, Billy," he exclaimed, "how are you doing?"

"Not bad, Harry. What about you?"

He laughed. "I'm on the worst losing streak of my life," he said. "Say, Billy, can you make any sense of this race? I don't know these Western horses."

I sat down beside him, looked at the *Form* and finally paid him back by picking him a winner.

7

View from the Guinea Stand

"Look at this work," the man said, tapping at the *Form* with a long, bony finger. "Blew out for this in thirty-three and four."

"Too fast," his friend said, shaking his head skeptically. "Much too fast for this kind."

"It means the horse is ready," said Bony Finger. "He'll murder this cheap field."

"It could also mean he leaves his race on the track in the morning," said the skeptic. "I don't like cheap horses working that fast the day before a race."

"These others in here," said Bony Finger, "they can't *run* as fast as this horse works."

"That's in the morning," said the skeptic. "Maybe he left his race on the track already."

"Ah, what do you know?"

"I know one thing only—I'm not putting a nickel on him."

"There ain't any nickel windows," said Bony Finger.
"Ha ha ha," the skeptic laughed mirthlessly.

Danny Velasquez works in a fenced-off corner of the
guinea stand, behind a narrow counter on which rests a
clipboard holding a long list of horse's names. Danny is
a trim little man wtih thick black hair, copper-colored
skin, and a good-humored, gentle-looking face. He's a
jockey who's been around a while but has never really
made it to the top, though he does still win races occasionally and he used to boot home regularly a top sprinting
mare named Time to Leave. But that was five or six years
ago and now Danny doesn't get to ride much in the afternoons anymore, so he's taken to supplementing his income
by acting as a spotter for the men who clock the workouts.
When I stopped at his perch, early on the morning of the
fifth day, I found him hunched into a windbreaker against
the chilly air and clutching a walkie-talkie in one hand; he
was leaning over the rail to exchange information with an
exercise boy bringing a chunky-looking horse back from a
test at a half mile.

"What'd you catch him in?" the boy asked, trying with
some difficulty to control his sweating, charged-up mount.

"They got him in fifty-four," Danny said.

"Fifty-four? How can a horse go so slow on this track?"
the boy said. "There must be a hole out there somewhere."

As horse and rider headed back toward the barns,
Danny held the walkie-talkie up to his ear and began to
scribble figures next to the names on his list. It was foggy
out there and not easy to identify the horses this morning,
so Danny had to really concentrate. The clockers work

from a perch high up above the main grandstand across the way and they depend on the spotter to identify many of the dozens of horses that appear on the track daily. Danny then feeds the results of the workouts back to the trainers, owners, and riders who may want to know how their horses did, or to confirm their own private clockings. What the spotter and the clockers come up with as accurate information is what shows up later in the *Racing Form* and is often the basis on which much money is wagered. Danny's part-time job is a thankless one, but it keeps him in touch with what's going on and occasionally that information can be very useful.

The guinea stand at Del Mar is a rickety-looking, green wooden platform looking down over the track at the head of the backstretch from where the sprint races start and adjacent to the main stable area. The origin of the term goes back a couple of hundred years of English racing history to a time when the stablehands were paid a guinea (about four dollars) a day and became called just that. Every racetrack has its guinea stand and in the afternoon, when the races are on, it will hold its small public of rooters, most of whom have something going that day but haven't the time to get over to the frontside to watch and/or make a bet. Generally, morning or afternoon, the guinea stands are rarely full, unless at post time a lot of money is at stake and somebody's big horse—a Cougar, a Secretariat, a Forego—is going. Then you'll see the guinea stands packed and you'll know that work back there among the long, low barns and walking rings has come to a brief, dramatic halt.

There was a big horse out on the track this morning,

Tizna, an older mare who's won over a half-million dollars and can go short or long, on any surface, and against top male horses as well as her own sex. "You have to beat her," is the way they put it when she's in a race and much of the time it's an impossibility. Her presence on the track for a work was drawing a lot of attention and Henry Moreno, her trainer, personally escorted her to the five-eighths pole, from where she'd begin to run. Moreno is a big man and he was mounted on a large white pony, so it was easy to follow their progress down the track. When Tizna broke away and began her run around the far turn, most of the observers around me momentarily forgot their own charges and watched her go. After she'd passed the finish line, I turned to look at Danny, who had his ear glued to the walkie-talkie again. "Fifty-nine flat," he said, smiling. In a race, of course, she'd go a lot faster than that, but it was the sort of work that indicated her fitness; she'd be ready to bear down later, when the big money was up and it counted.

"What a nice mare she is," a man in back of me said. "Only trouble is, you can't bet her most of the time, her price is so low."

"I never play her unless she's four to one or better," somebody else said. "Hell, that's when she likes to win. That mare can read the tote board, I swear!"

Right after the daily coffee break, at about eight-thirty, the sun emerged and began to take the chill out of the air. I sat down at last with the plastic cup full of coffee I'd brought back from the kitchen, leaned back, and spent the next hour just watching and listening. All around me, among the more casual watchers, trainers came and went, stopwatches in their hands, programs and condition books and *Forms* sticking out of their pockets. I knew more than a few of them: Charlie Whittingham, the richest and most successful of the locals, a tall, slightly stooped man with a shaved head, a small mouth and shrewd eyes, mentor of several dozen stalls full of topnotch horses; Les Holt, a thin, hunched-over veteran of the racing wars who's never had too many good horses but wins races; Dick Mulhall, a Fancy Dan with a lot of horses that rarely win but who has the best-looking girls working for him; Bobby Frankel, the boy genius from the East who wins more than anyone and doesn't mind how he does it; Murray Friedlander, a fine horseman who looks like a math teacher in a second-rate prep school; Lou Carno, courtly-looking, soft-spoken, not reluctant to discuss his chances, ever; Paul Falkenstein, a huge, obese, sloppily dressed veteran with the laugh and foul mouth of a carnival barker; Ed Gregson, one of the new breed, college-educated, boyishly handsome, an excellent tennis player as well as a man who sends out winners; and Hal King, who's never had too many good horses before but seems to be doing better and has the suffering face of a kindly pawnbroker. Trainers all, with credentials, high hopes, uncertain futures, and the fatal gift, so common at the track, for self-deception.

As I sat there, one of them, John Canty, walked quickly past me to corner Danny Velasquez, who used to ride Time to Leave for him. Canty is a short, slender, aging man with thin gray hair and the look of someone whose best times are behind him. He was excited now about the fact that one of the clockers had caught a horse of his working five furlongs in 59.2 seconds sometime earlier. He asked Danny to check it. "I had him in a minute and two," he said. "They can't clock a horse up there."

Danny took the walkie-talkie away from his ear. "I had the same time as them, John," he said.

"Well, you all missed him ten lengths," Canty snapped and walked quickly away. Obviously, he was unhappy over the knowledge that what he thought was the wrong figure would soon pop up in the *Form,* thus helping to shorten the odds on the horse when it came time for him to run. Trainers, most of them, like to bet and, if they could, they'd hide every workout, good and bad, from the public. Any edge you can get at the races, short of actually cheating, is an intrinsic part of the game.

I was still sitting there at ten o'clock, half-asleep, when the stand had emptied out and the sun felt hot on my shoulders. I stood up and stretched. Below me, the harrows were at work combing out the track and behind me, in the stable area, the last horses were being rubbed down and cooled out. It was that hour of the day when a lazy hush falls over the backstage world of the Thoroughbred. All that was left now was the racing itself. I went back to my motel to get some sleep.

"How can you like him?" the fat man asked indignantly. "How can you like any horse that shows a one-sixteen work? You got to love losin'."

"I ignore slow works," the young punk said. He had an enormous pair of Japanese binoculars that he wore around his scrawny neck like a yoke. "Slow works don't mean nothin'."

"Sure they do. They mean the horse can't run," the fat man said.

"Bullshit," the young punk told him. "How do you know what they were doing with the horse? He could've had one of them two-hundred-pound exercise boys they got here up on him, you don't know. They play games out here in the morning."

"Look," the fat man said, "I see a horse in here which don't show one work that's even OK, well, I can't play him."

"Shows how much you know," the young punk said. "I sit out there every morning and I got my glasses on all them pigs and I'm tellin' ya slow works don't mean nothin'. What I look for is *fast* works. That *means* something."

"So show me one fast work on this horse."

"They only got the last three in there," the young punk explained. "This horse has been workin' since the end of Santa Anita. Shit, he's had a thousand works. If he ain't ready now, he ain't never gonna be ready. And look at the breeding!"

"Breeding don't mean shit," the fat man said and spat angrily. "It's how they run that matters."

"I don't care if you die broke. It's *your* problem."

"Some problem," the fat man said. "The way you think, sonny, you'll be hockin' them big binocs before the week is out."

They separated to go and bet different horses in the race, neither of which finished in the money, but then it's hard to pick winners off workouts.

8

The Horses Run for Him

I was happy to see that Duke Wellington was still around. He wasn't getting many horses to ride anymore, an average of only one a day, but he seemed to be doing all right with what he had. In the second race of the fourth day, for instance, he brought an eighteen to one shot in second and on the next card he picked up another second with a seven to one shot. Maybe, if he kept that up, they'd start putting him on some really live mounts again. There are people at the track who bet on jockeys, but it's the horse that does the running. I wanted Duke to be successful, if only to prove me right about him, after all. I caught up to him by the backside racing office one morning that first week and asked him how he thought he was getting along.

"Oh, not bad," he said. "I'm trying to get on some good horses, but it's not so easy."

"Who's handling your book?"

"I don't have an agent," he said. "Why should I pay some guy twenty or twenty-five percent when I can get the mounts myself?"

"Can you?"

"I'm trying."

I pointed out to him that all the most active jockeys had agents, people who'd hustle around to the barns in the morning and the frontside in the afternoon, talking it up for their clients and getting the trainers to put them up on their horses. How could Duke be an exception? Why should he be any different?

"You think Shoemaker, Pierce, and those guys need agents?" he asked.

"They did once," I said. "Now they need them, I guess, to sort out the offers."

"Well, I think a little differently than most people."

I'd been wondering about that myself. Maybe that was part of the problem with Duke. Maybe that was why he hadn't yet made it to the top. If you're going to be a little different in a world as basically conservative as that of horse racing, then you'd better have something else going for you—at the very least a world of talent, and even that might not be enough. Not nearly.

I first saw him ride at Caliente, on a Sunday in March a few years ago when he brought home five winners in a row and made the local sports headlines. After that I began watching for him and I was at Santa Anita, a couple of weeks after the Mexican exploit, when he held a fifteen to one shot named Nigret's Pride together long enough to win the second race and make a friend of mine, who had bet on him, very happy. Later that same day I watched him miss by a nose on another horse, at eleven to one, that none of the wise guys around the track had given much of a chance. That was when I decided that H. K. Wellington, which is how they listed his name on the program, was a real race rider, the best looking young apprentice to come along in several years, and I decided to indulge my curiosity about him. Aside from the circumstance of size, how does anyone get to be a jockey, anyway?

I introduced myself to him in the backside kitchen a few days later, on the morning of the second day of the Hollywood Park meeting. He had been up since six-thirty and had been out on the track, working horses for various trainers, since seven. "I just blew out a little filly for a guy, but she's nothing," he explained. "Still, you have to do it. If you don't get out here early in the morning and work horses for people, you don't get the mounts. It's that simple." It was a little after eight and he wasn't scheduled to ride again till after the break, at about eight-thirty, so we sat down and had a cup of coffee together.

Harold Karl Wellington, sometimes called Duke by people with an oblique sense of history, looked very much at home already around the track. He's a nice-looking, dark-haired, well-proportioned young man and he was then just twenty-one years old. He's exactly five feet tall and weighed in every day at between 105 and 107 pounds, an ideal weight for a young rider at that stage of his career. More important, he was strong. It takes a lot of strength, in the legs and arms and hands, to break a thousand-pound Thoroughbred out of the starting gate, hustle him into position, settle him down, steer him around or through other horses, and drive hell-bent for the finish line, crouched up there over the horse's neck, the reins in one hand, the whip flailing in the other, getting the dirt kicked up into your face and all the while knowing that a loss of control can mean a bad spill and a serious injury, even death. In high school Wellington was on the wrestling team and later he'd studied karate with a Third Degree Black Belt named Victor Lipton, who then also happened to be his agent. "Karate is great training," Wellington said, "especially for things like anticipating moving into a hole before it's even there."

I got the impression, after talking to Wellington for a while, that everything he'd ever done and every minute of his time was directly connected to advancing him in his chosen career. And why not? Jockeys make pretty good money; the top two dozen earn annually over a hundred thousand dollars. Last year, out of some fifteen hundred active members of The Jockeys' Guild, about a hundred and fifty took home more than fifty thousand dollars. And below that level, a lot of riders simply make comfortable livings. Here in California, a jockey now gets thirty-five dollars and ten percent of the winning share of a purse. Today, at all major tracks, the winning purses, even in the cheapest races, come to several thousand dollars. No wonder it occurs to lots of strong little men (and now women, too) to take up riding careers.

It first occurred to Wellington during the summer of 1967, even though he'd never been on a horse before. Originally from San Francisco, where his father had been employed as a computer engineer, Wellington had just graduated with honors from an Orange County high school and had spent a semester at the University of Southern California, with the idea of following in his dad's footsteps. But he had some friends who hung around the track and they talked him into trying to become a rider. Vic Lipton probably had as much to do with it as anyone. He and Wellington had met over the form sheets at Del Mar, had begun handicapping winners together, and had become friends. Lipton, a stocky redhead in his late twenties, was obviously a born promoter. He gave Wellington karate lessons and talked racing to him. "I just had a feeling he'd make a good rider," Lipton told me later. "Physically he had everything going for him, in addition to the fact that he's a lot smarter than most of the people around the track. That's a big plus factor."

"That fall," Wellington said, "I went out to Rex Ellsworth's ranch in Chino and spent four months learning how to gallop and work horses. Then I went up to Golden Gate, when the meeting opened up there, and got a job exercising horses for an old-time trainer named Ace Gibson. He taught me a lot, about the way they run horses and also about the ways of the racetrack." The next summer he was back at Del Mar, where he went to work as an exercise boy for Johnny Longden. Longden had been a great jockey and he still liked to work a lot of his own horses. Wellington studied every move he made. He also got to ride some good horses himself in the mornings, which helped him supplement his income. "I was only making about four hundred dollars a month as an exercise boy," he said, "but I did a lot better than that betting on Mr. Longden's horses."

He'd stayed with Logden until the previous year, when

he went to work for Whittingham. Then, after the Oak
Tree meeting at Santa Anita in the fall, he decided the
time had come to start riding in races. "There were no
good bug boys around," he explained, meaning that there
was then, as there always is, a scarcity of the young apprentice riders a lot of trainers favor because, until they've
ridden forty-five winners and/or completed a minimum of
one year of apprenticeship, they receive weight allowances
ranging from eleven to five pounds on every horse they
ride. (These allowances are indicated in the program by
asterisks, known to horsemen as "bugs.") Racing is a sport
based largely on weight handicaps and a good bug boy
can be literally worth his lack of weight in gold. Wellington began shopping around for a place to prove himself.

The best market for his services, he decided, was to be
found at Caliente. "They'd had labor troubles getting the
Oak Tree meeting open and I'd heard they'd have more of
the same at Santa Anita later," he said. "I figured if I was
doing real well at Caliente I'd get a lot of good publicity,
especially with the big tracks closed." He contracted for a
first call on his services with a veteran trainer named L. L.
Marble and a couple of days later he appeared for the first
time in a pre-race post parade on the back of a poorly re-
garded plater named Jimquillo.

To everyone's amazement except Wellington's, Jimquillo
won the race. "Everybody thought I was out of it because
I was still dead last at the quarter pole," Wellington recalled. "But that horse came on and won like a champion."
After that, Marble put Wellington up on everything he had
in his barn and he discovered that, "if they had four legs
under them," his contract rider could bring them in. Soon

Wellington was averaging three or four winners a day and by the end of the year he topped the rider standings south of the border.

When, as he had anticipated, the Santa Anita opening that winter was delayed for a month by a labor dispute, Wellington began to receive a lot of attention. "I had come out of nowhere and nobody knew who I was," he said. "The day I rode my first race everybody thought I was a journeyman rider from England." It was a San Diego reporter who first tagged him with the name of Duke and it stuck. Wellington didn't mind, because he was in favor of anything that might do his career some good.

The next step, obviously, was the big time and that February, after Santa Anita finally got under way, Wellington and Lipton began hustling mounts at the big track during the week, though every weekend Wellington continued to ride at Caliente. He discovered very quickly that nobody at Santa Anita was overly impressed with his accomplishments and that he'd have to prove himself all over again in a much tougher league. "The other jocks tend to resent an intruder at first, though they respect you when you show some ability," he said. "I knew I still had a lot to learn. The caliber of horses and riders is so different from Caliente and up here. You have to ride a little bit different. You have to be in contention when you hit the quarter pole. At Caliente they ride loose and you can take a chance, bide your time. Not here. These guys ride tight, they don't let anybody through. And the action in the gate! Once or twice I almost got put over the rail. But each week I learn a lot more. Like when I lost a photo to Johnny Sellers. I studied the movies of that race and I saw how

Sellers flicked the nose of his horse up with his whip as we hit the finish line and got it up to win. I've done that myself a couple of times since and won races with it."

By the time Santa Anita ended, Wellington had ridden nine winners, picked up shares of a couple of dozen other purses, and established a demand for his services. It looked very much as if he stood on the threshold of a big career. I fully expected him to make it.

I remember sitting high in the stands later that same morning, after we'd finished our coffee, and watching Wellington work a horse for John Pappalardo, a genial, bulky man who has been around race tracks in one capacity or another most of his life. Pappalardo had used Wellington before and he was high on his ability. He sat next to me and predicted a bright future for him. "He used to look terrible on a horse, but now he's screwed down real tight," he said. "Anyway, it isn't how you look on a horse that counts. The worst-looking rider I ever saw was Shoemaker, when he started at Golden Gate years ago. I saw him fall off a horse twice in the same race. Now, this kid, the horses run for him. It's in his hands, that's the story on a bug rider. Wellington's got the hands."

That afternoon I caught up to Wellington again just before the last race of the day. He and Lipton were standing together at the clubhouse bar and I asked both of them how they thought things were going. "I know I'm going to win here," Wellington told me. "I know I still do a lot of things wrong and that I have a lot to learn, but I have the intangible. My main strength is that horses really run for me. There are horses that'll run for me and no one else. I know what to do on a horse. I watch the other riders. I've watched them all, I've studied their every move. Pincay, he's the most powerful rider. He's very powerful with the stick and he can hold a horse together very well. Shoemaker's the best judge of pace. Sellers and Pierce, they're great riders, especially at a distance. Campas is great in the gate and so is Velasquez. Lambert is very impressive in the gate. I watch these men. I still have trouble with some things, like trying to hold a horse together and switching sticks at the same time. Inexperience is my main disadvantage."

"But brainwork is where we have the edge," Lipton told me. "We've made a careful study of everything. We know who the smart people are on this track and we're going to move with them."

Wellington looked suddenly thoughtful and a little somber. "I lose my bug on December 7th," he said, "and that's the moment of truth. I don't want to be just a sensational apprentice and then drop out of sight like so many of them do. I want to be an all-around competent rider because I plan to be here for a while. And to do that I'll take chances. Some jockeys won't take chances anymore. They're rich, so why should they? Maybe in ten years, when I'm a millionaire, I'll be more settled, like some of these other guys, but right now I'm hungry."

So what happened to Duke's career, all of his big plans? What happened between him and Lipton, whom I'd been seeing around the L.A. tracks but usually by himself and on his way to and from the betting windows? "It's a personal matter," Duke told me that morning in Del Mar. "I don't want to talk about it." Later I heard that they'd had a falling out over a woman, but the details seemed only ordinarily sordid and not worth harping on. But what about the great career? Wellington had been riding the Southern California circuit for several years now and clearly he was not making it in the way we'd both imagined he might that first morning I talked to him, when he was hungry and full of self-confidence.

"I'm still hungry and I can ride," Wellington said, "but the people here, I don't know. . . ." His voice trailed away and he looked beyond me toward the barns. "Anyway, I'm going around to see some people, try to get some live mounts. But if things don't break, I may just go someplace else. I want to go to Hawaii."

"They have racing there?"

"I don't know," he said, "but I've never been there. Maybe, this fall, I'll go on down to New Orleans. I can get good horses to ride down there. Then, well, I'm not sure yet." He suddenly spotted a trainer he wanted to talk to and left me. "Nice seeing you again," he called out. "I'll be around later, if you want to talk to me again."

A couple of weeks after this conversation, Wellington left Del Mar. During that time he received very few riding assignments and brought in no winners. I discussed him one day with an old friend of mine up in the press box. "Duke?" my friend said, with a smile. "He's funny. He looks so bad on a horse and he thinks he's the greatest."

"He can win races."

"Maybe," my friend said, "but the ego on him! That first year he came up he pissed everybody off. He was going around telling everyone how great he was. He even went up to Shoemaker and told him to watch out, that soon he'd be number one and Shoe'd better be ready for him. Well, now he knows. You've got to watch yourself in this business if you're a jock, no matter how good you are. Where's Bill Hartack today? You can't go around telling everybody how good you are, because, in the long run, you're only as good as the horses under you. You notice even Shoe and Pierce and the others, they're out here in the mornings to work horses for people and they're pretty nice to *everybody*. They don't go around telling everyone how great they are. Duke's problem is his mouth. You know what Shoemaker said to him when Wellington walked up to him that day? 'Kid,' he said, 'save your money.' "

9

Stuck in the Gate and Elsewhere

A funny thing happened on the ninth day of the meeting. A horse called Monter, entered in the eighth and feature race at a mile on the turf, got left in the starting gate. Here's how it was officially reported in the chart of the race published in the *Form* the following day: "MONTER became fractious and reared just as start was taken then had to be strongly handled while thrashing wildly in gate and unseated his rider resulting in his never leaving gate. The connections of MONTER called stewards lodging protest into start. Inquiry was posted while films were reviewed then official went up with ruling being horse caused his own trouble."

This version was not embraced by a large portion of the crowd that had backed Monter down to seven to two in the odds. The horse had been a hot tip all over the track and several of my friends had bet him heavily. The inquiry into the start, in fact, had been the result of a loudly vocal protest on the part of a small, angry mob of about forty people who set up a fearful din in the clubhouse. Nor did the findings of the inquiry please this group, especially when the stewards neglected to show films over the TV monitors of a head-on shot of the goings-on in the gate just before the start of the race. One plunger, who claimed he had bet three thousand dollars on the horse, screamed so loudly that eventually he had to be carried off the premises in handcuffs by the security guards and spent a few ranting and raving hours in the local cooler. For a while it even looked as if the losers might get up a little posse to storm the upstairs Bastille, where the stewards wisely chose to remain barricaded and impregnable in their officially sanctioned stance of incorruptible virtue.

The owners of Monter, however, persisted in demanding to see films of the race, especially after their rider, Raul Cespedes, was heard to remark that an assistant starter had held the horse's head and refused to let go when the gate opened. This theory was quickly dispelled when the stewards did show complete films the following morning and the owners apologized publicly to starter Bob Yerian for having cast dark aspersions on his skills, as well as on the honesty of his staff. What the films showed was a horse that went absolutely wild when enclosed into his tiny stall within the gate and who chose to rear and turn his head just as Yerian pressed the button that electronically opened the doors. The idea behind a good start to a race is to release the animals all at the same time, but most often that turns out to be an impossibility. Horses have a way of acting up always at the wrong moment and not even the best starter in the world can guarantee good behavior and a perfect break from as many as twelve fractious beasts loaded and locked into a row of tiny stalls and expected to stand there, alertly but quietly, until they can be suddenly sprung into the clear. An ideal start to any race is almost as impossible to achieve as the track handicapper's assumption that he can guarantee a blanket photo finish simply by assigning horses in a race different weights. Horse racing is many things, but it will never be an exact science.

I went around to talk to Bob Yerian early one morning, a few days later. He was out on the track with several of his assistant starters, including his twenty-one-year-old son, helping various trainers to run their horses through the schooling gate, which is merely a smaller model of the larger one used in the afternoons. When I got there, he was helping to load a spirited two-year-old filly named Flashy Pass into a stall while her trainer, a tall, lanky Kentuckian named Tom Blincoe, sat by on his pony and watched. "She's better now, isn't she, Bob?" Blincoe said, watching the filly shift nervously on her feet inside the stall. "She used to be spooky as hell in there."

After a few seconds, the gate was opened manually by one of Yerian's assistants and Flashy Pass, ridden by a pretty young exercise girl, walked nervously but cleanly out of her stall. "She's better, all right," Yerian said. "She's coming along fine." Blincoe looked pleased and rode away after his horse, which was scheduled to work three furlongs in preparation for a race later in the meet.

Bob Yerian is a solidly built, middle-aged man with a thick mop of gray hair and the ruddy look of someone who has spent most of his life outdoors. He doesn't ruffle easily and his maner is quiet, even subdued, though he's obviously respected by his crew and the horsemen he deals with on a daily basis. He grew up in Montana, where he had a brother in the horse business, and he himself began as a trainer. "I went broke twice training my own horses," he told me. "The races were cheap and the purses were small back then, but it was an education." He moved to California in 1949 and went to work as an assistant starter at the northern tracks, then became a head starter in 1967. Every summer now he comes south for the Del Mar meeting before heading north again in the early fall. I gathered from talking to him that he enjoyed his work. "Oh, sure," he said. "It keeps me busy and around horses."

He has seen the animals at their worst and, in fact, keeps a long list of bad actors he wants to run through his schooling gate. "We had a maiden filly in here the other day that tried to dive over the gate," he said. "Earlier today we had Tuxedo, that horse of Tom Pratt's. He likes to flip over backwards. Some horses just never take to the gate, but it helps if you school them enough times. The good trainers will bring their horses by here all the time before taking them out on the track to work or to gallop without having to be told to, like Tom Blincoe. He'll put six, eight horses a day through the gate. The first few times we just walk them through, to get them used to it. When a horse gets to know what the gate is all about, it shouldn't take any more than five seconds to load him. After they're used to that, we break them out of the main gate a few times, so they'll know what's expected of them in a race."

Not only are there some horses, however, that never learn; there are some whose education is limited. I once bet some money at Santa Anita on a colt named Harbor Hauler, who obviously took only his early schooling totally to heart. The day I risked money on him, he simply walked out of his stall when the bell rang and sauntered out onto the track with the unconcern of an aged passenger rising from his deck chair to have a minor go at the cruise shuffleboard tournament. The jockey sat on his back, banging away at him in vain, though after what seemed to be no more than half an hour Harbor Hauler did manage to rouse himself into a rheumatic lope. The stewards mercifully banished him from the local racing scene, but not before my wager had disappeared forever into the maws of the mutuals.

"The worst gate horse here used to be that filly Coradon," Yerian said. "She wanted to dive through or under or over, she'd try anything. She's Tom's horse and he's been patient with her. Now she'll actually stand still long enough so we can get her out with the other horses, but we always load her last, so she won't go crazy waiting." He looked suddenly thoughtful. "It's funny about trainers," he said. "You'd think they'd be eager to get all the schooling they can for their horses, but some of these fellows, I have to go after them to get them to bring their horses here."

As we stood by the gate and talked, Rudy Campas rode up on Joy to the World, a filly trained by Willis Reavis that was running in a stakes race that very afternoon. Reavis's exercise boy Dick Schmidt came up beside us and watched Yerian and his men maneuver her carefully into the gate. "She's weird in there," Schmidt said. "One time she'll stand good, the next day she'll get to rockin' back and forth and get herself all worked up. It don't help her none." No, I thought, nor the poor wretches like myself who might actually risk money on her.

This morning, however, Joy to the World seemed to relish her time in the gate. She stood quietly in her stall and emerged a few seconds later to jog away up the track, Campas high up in the irons with a good tight hold on her. In fact, she behaved so well that later in the day I bet on her to win her race and watched her come quickly out of the gate, then tire and finish a distant third. In her previous public effort, she'd acted up, broken poorly, and won coming from behind. Reavis hadn't liked her chances the day she won, but had told me before I'd gone off to meet Yerian that she'd be "real tough to beat today." Why are horses so goddamned inconsistent, anyway?

I spent the rest of the morning till nine o'clock watching Bob Yerian and his men run green and fractious horses through this same procedure over and over again, then I walked him back toward the racing office. "Oh, the horses aren't always to blame for the way they act, you know," he said in reply to my query about Monter. "Usually it's the people who do something crazy. They put closed blinkers on that horse, so he couldn't see. When we put him in the gate, he naturally panicked. As for what the rider said about my man holding him, he must have bet a few bucks himself." Yerian smiled. "I'm in one of those jobs where it's hard to be a hero and there are lots of folks who think I'm in on some kind of plot or other. They shout at me when they see me heading for the gate and

they want to know whose turn it is this time. People are funny . . ."

The next time Coradon ran she was her usual edgy, intractable self, lathered to the ears with sweat and making difficulties for her rider, the veteran Milo Valenzuela. They had forgotten to put blinkers on her in the saddling stall and these were added at the gate just before she was loaded, though no announcement of this important equipment change was made to the crowd. They bet on her anyway, backing her down from six to one to two to one at post time. Bob Yerian, all dressed up now in a tie and jacket, stood alone in his little tower just in front of the gate, watching his crew work to get the horses to stand still and face front on all four feet long enough to get them away cleanly. The men snapped instructions and warnings to each other as they worked with the animals and from time to time Yerian told one of them to get a horse's head up or turned front, then—*wham!*—the gate burst open and the horses exploded at full speed into the clear, the long run to the turn ahead of them and a great cloud of dirt clods spewed out behind them, while in the background the roar of the crowd rose like a curtain of sound to envelop them.

Coradon broke beautifully this time. She quickly took the lead and won going away, after setting a bristling early pace that cooked all of her main rivals. When Bob Yerian climbed down from his tower, he seemed more than usually pleased.

He rode back to the stands in an open convertible limousine and when he stepped out of the car, the first voice he heard was that of an angry man who leaned out of his seat in the clubhouse to shout, "Hey, starter, what did they give that filly to make her run like that? A little moose juice?"

10

An Off-Day with the Dreamers

"You mean they got a laundry here?" the old man asked. "I didn't know they had a laundry."

"Oh, sure," I told him. "You just bring it by the desk, as I'm doing, and they send it out."

"Dry-cleaning, too?"

"Of course." I handed the girl my bundle of dirty clothes and looked at the old man, who was leaning against the counter and had apparently been chatting with her. He was thin, but with a prominent pot belly, and he had an evidently perfect set of false teeth that he kept resolutely clamped around a large cigar during our entire conversation. It was early in the morning, a few minutes before seven, but he was already well-groomed, his thick, curly gray hair combed straight back and cheeks aglow with some heavily scented after-shave lotion. He was elegantly attired for the resort life in a gaudy short-sleeved sports shirt, out of which his arms protruded like wizened celery stalks, purple slacks and black loafers. I took him for a small-time movie producer.

"I was thinking of driving back up to L.A. today," the old man said thoughtfully. "Usually, on Tuesdays here, I go back to L.A. and pick up clean clothes. But maybe, if they got a laundry here, I might stay. A cleaner's, you said?" I explained to him that these services were not performed at the motel itself, but in the town of Del Mar; it took a couple of days at most. "You mean there's a town? Where's the town?" the old man asked.

"This is your first trip down?"

"Oh, no," the old man said. "I come here every year since they opened this place. Five, six years, I forget."

I stared at him. The Winners Circle Lodge, where we were staying, is a few hundred yards off the freeway and nestled up against the stable area, from where the smell of the horses wafts on the prevailing winds from the ocean over the pool area. Beyond the grandstand and the front-side of the track itself is the beach and the town of Del Mar, not more than a mile or so away. I had a hard time making myself believe that this courtly old man in his fancy resort clothes had been coming to Del Mar for the racing every year without ever having done anything but divide his time between the Lodge and the track. I expressed my skepticism to him and he simply puffed once or twice on his cigar and shrugged. "It's a nice little town," I elaborated. "Since they don't race here on Tuesdays, why don't you drive in and look around?"

"What's to see?"

I told him. Del Mar is small and pleasant. It has quiet, narrow residential streets with modest wooden houses tucked behind front lawns and, nearer the beach, clusters of elegant-looking, expensive condominiums. The coastal highway runs through the business center, a stretch of two or three blocks with a small shopping mall and a row of attractive stores, including a couple of boutiques, catering mostly to the summer tourist trade. Unlike its neighboring towns to the north, Del Mar has fairly strict zoning laws and has made some effort to defend itself from commercial advertisers, excessive real-estate speculation, and a consequent conversion to the honkey-tonkism that characterizes the rest of the beach communities between it and Los Angeles. I recommended a visit to this tiny haven of civilization as a way of making the time pass on Tuesdays, the one day of the week the horses don't run here.

The old man heard me out, but seemed uninspired. "Listen," he said, "I lived in New York City for forty years and I never went up the Empire State Building or went out to that statue they got out there in the harbor. Then I lived in Miami for twelve years, but I never went on no boats. I don't know towns. I know racetracks."

Outside in the pool area, later that morning, I found The Mole. He was stretched out in a deck chair, where he had probably spent the night (The Mole is a stickler for saving money), and was surrounded by the tangible evidences of his more recent burrowing—stacks of *Forms* and charts and condition books and thick pads across whose lined pages mysterious combinations of numerals maneuvered and scrambled for space in tangled ranks. The Mole believes that horse racing is a science to which a formula can be applied that will guarantee success. He has lived with this conviction for thirty-two of his approximately forty years of perseverance on this planet and it has ruined his life. Even worse, it has shattered the faith of his elders. The Mole is a nice Jewish boy from a nice Jewish family back in Minneapolis who actually made it all the way through school to become a C.P.A., but he has never practiced. At the age of about eight, he discovered his real life's work, which is the application of systematic arithmetical calculations to the improvement of the breed, with the idea of one day producing a mathematically guaranteed panacea impervious to the vagaries and odd inconsistencies that habitually plague the world of the Thoroughbred. The Mole is a dreamer, but it is not a dream that enchants his tribe, for of what profit is it to a matriarch or an elder to point him out to friends and say, "That's my son the horse-player." The Mole, however, remains impervious to disapproval and almost immune to reality. He survives by taking occasional menial jobs in the stable area, where he has labored at mucking out stalls and hot-walking cripples, and always seems to be able to put enough money together to stay in pursuit of the dream, though in thirty-two years of concentrated effort he hasn't gained an inch on it. I asked him, as usual, how he was doing.

"I made one big bet yesterday and won," he said. "I've always liked Del Mar."

A big bet for The Mole might be six dollars, but I let that pass. "You're winning here?" I inquired.

"I lost some the first few days, but everything's coming around now. I should have a good meet," he said. "I've only made seven bets so far."

"Don't you find that boring?"

"Boring?"

"Sitting there, day after day, race after race, until at last, when all the numbers come together, you can make one bet?"

"It's the only way to win."

"I know all about that, Mole. I have one observation to make."

"What's that?"

"There's such a thing as too much knowledge."

He stared at me in quiet amazement, his large brown eyes blinking sadly through the thick lenses of his horn-rimmed glasses. I had blasphemed. "What do you mean?" he said. "Knowledge is everything."

I knew he would say something like that, but I had no answer for him. There is nothing to be gained by challenging the faith of those whose lives are enclosed in cocoons of dogma. I wished him luck, which he clearly felt was superfluous and irrelevant to his needs, and walked away. The Mole ultimately depresses me, because there is something of his pitiful wrongheadedness buried within the psyche of every gambler and it sometimes frightens me a little, for there but for the grace of God or a good analyst go . . . more than a few of us.

Everyone who goes to the races or who gambles anywhere finds himself at some point dreaming of some way to beat the odds. Casinos all over the world are full of little old women hunched over columns of numbers and palsied men consulting little black books before every turn of the wheel or throw of the dice. Most of these people, like The Mole, have spent years, some entire lifetimes, attempting to develop some sort of system or method of gambling that will enable them to live in luxury the rest of their lives without having to work. Their faith is absolute and touching, like that of Ponce de Leon in his quest for the Fountain of Youth, and has just about as much chance of being rewarded. This is because the only sure way to win is a mindless system called the Martingale, which calls for the bettor to double up on even-money bets after every loss.

There are only two troubles with the Martingale: to make it work you'd have to be as rich as J. Paul Getty and you'd have to persuade the casino to remove the house limit on any single bet. Starting with a dollar, a losing streak of ten wagers would find you risking one thousand twenty-four dollars. And should you lose that one, your next bet would have to be two thousand forty-eight dollars. Should you win either test, you'd show a net profit of one dollar. It doesn't take a genius to figure out that the mathematics of the thing are insane.

There are many, many other systems, but they all ultimately come up against the terrible reality of the house percentage, which is always against the bettor and ranges from a low of less than one in certain situations at Craps to twenty or more at such sucker lures as slot machines and lotteries. At the track, it's the fifteen to twenty percent cut out of every dollar wagered. Casinos and racetracks are not charitable institutions. Every time you make a bet in them you are bucking what can be defined as a minus expectation and there is no way to add up a lot of minuses to make a plus. Unless you are like the man in the old joke who thinks the chain stores lose money on every item they sell but show a profit because they sell so many of each.

A couple of years ago I came across a chap named Alexander Somerset, an English horseplayer who, like most of us, has spent a lifetime trying to win at the races. Somerset started off his career at the age of thirteen by winning his first six bets and he had what he thought at the time was a foolproof system. It was to bet on the horse with the longest tail. Later in life, after the usual parade of disillusionments, he became, like The Mole, a scientific plunger and money manager, which, if you have a good head for figures, some knowledge of horses, and iron self-control, can yield rewards, at least over a not inconsiderable period of time. Somerset estimated at one point that there were five thousand two hundred and thirty-eight different facts and figures to take into account in any one race, which involved him in computations that were time-consuming and staggering in their complexity. During one stretch, for instance, he piled up a profit of two hundred pounds (about five hundred dollars), at the small price of nearly ruining his marriage and being fired from his job. This is where science and logic will ultimately lead you.

Somerset, however, never lost his capacity to dream. He was brought to my attention by an article he wrote for an English magazine named *Lords,* in which he actually touted a new sure-fire system, the Hampton, named after one James Hampton. It was, according to Somerset, "the most boring, the least time-consuming, the most simple and, so far in my own experience, the most reliable system I've ever played." Somerset asked the reader if he wanted an assured income of about thirty pounds a week for the rest of his life and then proceeded to explain how the Hampton system would provide it:

The Hampton system is basically a sophisticated version of the doubling up system and it works this way. Let's assume you want to win an average of one pound a race for every race of every meeting you back. So on the first race you bet whatever the odds determine to win exactly one pound. If you lose, then on the second race you want to win one pound plus the one pound you didn't win on the first race, plus the stake money you bet. If you lose again you then want to win the three pounds plus the stake money bet on the first two races. And you go on like this until you have a winner, and then start all over again. . . . The beauty of it is that it doesn't matter what odds your winner finally comes up with because you've bet enough to make up all your losses plus all your stake money.

The trick, Somerset was quick to point out, was finding the winner, because a dozen losing races in a row could lead you to having to put down very sizeable amounts of money, up to five hundred times the original wager. So Somerset recommended that the bettor select an expert handicapper and follow him, never once deviating from his standard, with the fervor of a crusader in the wake of Peter the Hermit. Such devotion, Somerset assured us, would be rewarded and he went on to recount that he and four friends had formed a syndicate, that they never went to the track but did it all by phone (bookies are legal in England), and that they were each banking about thirty pounds a week. "It needs half an hour in the morning at breakfast," said Somerset, "and then anything from two to twelve calls in the afternoon—usually, I confess, done by my secretary who gets ten percent for her efficiency." The guy made it sound like an annuity or a form of Social Security.

At the time I read this piece, I had just emerged from a disastrous closing visit of two weeks at Del Mar and was girding myself, with diminished resources and confidence, to tackle the nags at the short fall meeting at Santa Anita known as Oak Tree. I decided to cut my own betting down drastically till I got my touch back and to amuse myself by applying the Hampton system, but on paper only, to this meet.

I immediately ran into one enormous complication, which was that the system could not be applied at any American track without tremendous capital risk, because handicappers tend to pick favorites and too many favorites go off at odds of even money or less. (In Europe the favorite is rarely odds-on and often pays four to one or better.) Any string of odds-on selections running out would demolish my theoretical bankroll. So I decided to limit myself to selections paying three to one or better and to try for a hundred dollars a day, or a profit of about ten dollars a race.

The adapted system broke down the very first day, with a net loss of eighty-one dollars. For the twenty days of the meeting it showed losses on eleven days totalling eight hundred and forty-eight dollars and profits on nine totalling about nine hundred and sixty-four dollars, for a net of a hundred and sixteen, not quite as much as I'd have raked in simply by going on Welfare. In its virgin form,

however, the system showed profits for the first eighteen
days and for every day but the fatal nineteenth. For
nineteen days, then, the total profits came to about two
thousand dollars, but the one losing day was a shocker—an
even sixteen hundred and twenty-nine dollars. Net profit
for the whole meet: about three hundred and seventy
dollars.

Nevertheless, I might then and there have become a
devotee of the Hampton system, if it hadn't been for a
couple of major side factors. I had been using as my expert
Bob Hebert, the pleasant and supremely able handicapper,
now retired, for the *Los Angeles Times*. Hebert, however,
like most of his colleagues, tends to pick favorites and the
favorites at this Oak Tree Meet did unusually well, winning about forty percent of the time, as compared to a
norm of about thirty percent. What if there had been two
losing days instead of one? Hebert, like all handicappers,
professional or amateur, has his losing streaks. I consider
them all less reliable sources of winners than my own head,
if only because I have the added advantage of being able
to pick my horse at the last minute, after having considered such contributing factors as weight shifts, changes of
jockey, the look of the horse (is he bandaged? is he sweating? does his coat shine?), and a hundred other considera-
tions denied to pros like Hebert, who have to make their
selections in time for the early editions.

More important, as far as I was concerned, was the fact
that I refound my own handicapping touch at Oak Tree
and came up with forty-nine winners and a net profit for
the month of about a thousand dollars. I've told myself

that someday I'm going to look up Mr. Somerset when I get to England again. I'll lay odds he's tapped out.

Off-days for the dreamers at the track can seem interminable. I spent most of my time reading or making notes for this book. My friend Gary spent his leisure hours cavorting on the beach. Gary is in his late thirties, but he still plays a pretty fair game of vollyball. I watched him at it one Tuesday from the open terrace of The Fire Pit, a bar and restaurant next to the lifeguard station at the main public beach. He was competing on better than even terms with men ten years or more younger than he. Against the slope of the dunes beside the net, a half-dozen Del Mar nymphets sat combing out their long blond tresses or lay stretched out to the sun in their all but invisible bikinis and string suits. Volleyball, too, has its groupies. From here the beach stretches visibly for miles in both directions, the long, slow rollers full of surfers and swimmers, the sands dotted by mid-week vacationers, groups of teenagers, mothers with small children, and some of the backside people enjoying their only full day of relaxation during the racing week. Along the edge of the water, joggers pounded past, running barefoot on the hard sand. Beside me, at the next table, two dilapidated-looking men in wrinkled street clothes, failed dreamers, were reliving the nightmare of the previous day, obviously too crushed by the experience to want to share in the pleasures of the sunny afternoon.

"At three to five Shoemaker stiffs me," one of them said. "I mean, why can't that guy ever win one for me? If I bet

on him, he loses. But if I don't, he kills me. Why don't he
retire and save us all this anguish?"

"He can't retire," his companion said. "He's broke."

"Broke? Shoemaker? He's a millionaire ten times over."

"That's your opinion, friend. I hear he made bad invest-
ments and he's got this broad that bets with both hands, a
big loser."

"He's married, ain't he?"

"That's the broad."

"So that's why he don't retire. Some goddam woman.
He's damn near fifty, ain't he? He ought to hang it up."

"Yeah, well . . . what are you going to do?"

Gary came over after his game and joined me. He sat
down, still panting, and ordered coffee and a side of
bacon. "You're washing out pretty good," I said. "Aren't
you about ready to retire? Like Shoemaker?"

"Shoemaker? I need this," he answered, grinning. "I put
on all kinds of weight during the winter, but Del Mar gets
me in shape. By the end of the season, I've taken off ten
pounds and I'm really feeling good."

Gary is a math teacher in a Los Angeles public school,
a perfect profession for a horseplayer. He's usually through
by early afternoon, which enables him to get to Santa
Anita and Hollywood Park during the working months,
and then there are the long summer vacations that he can
devote full-time to Del Mar. He has a reputation for being
able to pick winners and has been known to win sizeable
amounts of money with shrewd bets. Essentially, he's a
speed handicapper, which means that he likes to bet on
horses that show fast works or have displayed a marked
ability to get out in front in races or have shown they can

run really fast at one stage or another of their afternoon efforts. Gary's success depends entirely on his ability not only to pick out the best speed horse in a race but to estimate exactly when that speed is about to be put to profitable use. He is not so much a dreamer as a calculator. At least that's how he thinks of himself. I asked him how he was faring so far.

"Terrible," he said. "They play too many games down here."

"Gary, are you implying that the racing isn't honest?"

"Implying? Hell, I'm *telling* you, straight out." He launched into his favorite theme, which he can sound on at length and is always a good clue to how he's doing in the daily confrontation with the parimutuals. When Gary is winning, he can sit silently for hours, looking like a cat after a prolonged bout with the catnip canister. "The real trouble is the trainers," he said. "It's not the horses."

"What about the jockeys?"

"It's the trainers," he insisted. "The biggest bunch of dumbbells in the world. You know I used to own horses, don't you? Well, I had one criterion for picking my trainer. If he could write his own name without misspelling it, I figured his I.Q. was well above the average. I had a friend named Doc Rains who used to own horses, too. He died last winter, you didn't hear? Probably had a stroke after watching some trainer cock up his horse. Well, anyway, he hated them even more than I do. You ever heard a trainer admit he made a mistake with a horse? And they always have a million excuses for blowing it. They ought to have a thing in the *Form*—you know, where they list the horses' names and make some comment like 'Sharp now' or 'Ready

for a smasher' or 'In good hands'—well, when the horse is
trained by one of the major morons, the comment ought to
read 'In hands idiot' or 'Horse trying, trainer isn't,' something like that. Anyway, old Doc Rains, he used to put
those dumbbells on, tell them all kinds of ludicrous things,
and they never knew whether to believe him or not. One
time, last year, I was at a party with him here and he got
going on how the only way to ensure honest racing would
be to have the horses ridden by monkeys and trained by
gorillas. But then he got to thinking about it and he realized it would never work and some trainer in the room
asked him why not and Doc said, 'Because some imbecile
would have to train the gorillas.' "

"Gary, how much are you losing?"

"Too much," he said. "Much too much. I used to like
Del Mar, but now. . . . I may just stick to volleyball for a
while."

He might, too. Right up until a couple of hours before
post time the following day; Gary likes to get to the track
early. He's a dreamer, too, like the rest of us.

11

Snow White and All the Dwarfs

"Yes," jockey Barbara Jo Rubin once told an interviewer, "there's something pretty exciting about having one thousand pounds of Thoroughbred horse between your knees, going a mile a minute."

I'd already heard a lot about Mary Bacon before I ever saw her. She was the only girl jockey on the grounds and was reputedly the best of the female race riders. I'd also read somewhere about how she'd recently joined the Ku Klux Klan, which seemed a singularly dumb thing to do but didn't connect to me in any significant way. Then, on opening day at Del Mar, I'd seen her ride in the first race on the card. It was a mile gallop for cheap claiming horses and she had brought her mount, Silver Salute, in third. Not a great achievement, but it had impressed me because I knew the horse well. Silver Salute was a five-year-old gray gelding adept at breaking hearts; he ran late in sprints and tired at a distance and won an average of once a year. Mary Bacon wouldn't let him quit. She managed somehow to keep him going and picked up a piece of the purse. A lot of other jocks, including some of the most celebrated ones, wouldn't have tried that hard.

Like most horseplayers, I've never liked girl jockeys. Most of them simply aren't strong enough to get the best out of such large, dumb, and unpredictable animals as Thoroughbreds. I knew that Mary Bacon had won a lot of races back East, but that didn't mean much to me. I want to see them ride first, whatever their sex, before I risk any money at the windows.

Mary Bacon came up to the press box later that afternoon and gave an interview to the assembled cynics there. She knew she was entering a male-chauvinist bastion and she dressed for the occasion. Her platinum-blond hair was pulled back into a ponytail under a cowboy hat with a long feather stuck into the band and her deep tan was set off by big gold-hoop earrings. In her lap she held a Dr. Seuss doll she introduced to the boys as "Mr. Cat" and she was sucking a cherry lollipop. "You guys used to think I was National Velvet, now I'm a monster," she told the gentlemen of the press.

It was her way of denying the KKK story. She'd gone to one meeting, she explained, as a kind of lark, but the newspapers had blown it up into something monstrous. All she wanted to do was ride horses and the only reason she talked to the press at all was because she knew the boys would write about her anyway and she might as well try and protect herself. Truth was in lending, not in life.

I liked her immediately. She seemed fearless and her answers, delivered in a flat southwestern drawl, cut through the uneasy, clumsy questioning of the press-box boys like a meat cleaver through lard. "This political crap is over," she concluded. "I'm here to win races. It's tough at Del Mar because it's late in the season, a lot of the horses are hurting and the fields are short. For any new rider coming in, and I'm new out here, it's a slow move-up. The fact that I'm a woman is just a fact, nothing else. So what if I look like Snow White with the Seven Dwarfs out there in the paddock? When I win a few races here, I'll just be one of the boys again."

The second time I saw her was at one of Pat Rogerson's Sunday brunches. Rogerson is a tall, good-looking Irishman in his early forties who writes a daily column for the *Racing Form* and is cursed with the sometimes fatal gift of his race for blarney. He has a large, jolly Italian wife, a big brood of large, noisy children and a penchant, perhaps as a consequence of the daily pressures upon him, for the sauce, another well-established Gaelic malediction. He writes a little too easily and fluently, is somewhat cavalier with facts, is adept at inventing quotes (or "recreating conversations," as he puts it), but turns out reams of stuff every day that is, on the whole, very readable, especially in a newspaper as exploitive of its staff and inept and cowardly in its editing as the *Form*. What he does best, however, is preside over his public brunches, which anyone can attend for a quite reasonable fee of three or four dollars and to which he invites a panel of guests from the professional world of racing, who talk on various aspects of the sport and then are asked to make their selections for each

race on that day's program. Rogerson is the chief interviewer and master of ceremonies, a chore he performs with
the brassy, good-humored aplomb of a host on one of those
TV game shows full of greedy, shrieking housewives. After
all, the guests at his brunches are there to get inside tips
from the pros, not to learn anything of lasting significance.
At Del Mar these functions were held at the Winners
Circle Lodge, out in the open under beach umbrellas set
up beside the tennis courts. At the first one I attended
Rogerson's guests were Tom Blincoe, Dushan Lazovich,
the handicapper for the *San Diego Union,* and Mary
Bacon.

I sat down with my eggs and coffee across from a quarrelling middle-aged husband and wife. At least I assumed
they'd been quarrelling, because the first thing I heard was
her saying to him, "I don't want to hear your selections.
I'm going to stick to my own." To which he replied, somewhat obliquely but with the sullen look of a man already
deep in the hole, "Sonofabitch, the only people doing good
at this meeting are the stewards." Horseplayers don't look
well in the sunlight either, I realized. I put on my shades
just as someone in back of me observed, "The melon here
is odds-on, but it's eight to five you get tepid coffee." I'm
addicted to this kind of talk and could have listened to it
all day, but just then Pat Rogerson seized the microphone
and introduced his three guests, who were seated on an
improvised dais facing the hundred or so paying brunchers.

What the panelists had to say that morning proved to
be only mildly interesting and of no use whatever to the
bettors. Blincoe happened to have three horses entered
that day and informed us that he especially liked the

chances of the first two, though all three were to run out of the money. He also touted everyone onto a horse called E. Eddie Edwards in the seventh as "the lock of the meet" and suggested we all plunge on him. (Fortunately, I ignored this advice and had the satisfaction of watching E. Eddie Edwards come in third, which only went to prove an old racetrack saw of mine that trainers are notoriously poor handicappers, primarily because they know only their own horses.) When challenged by someone to explain why he thought his horses would run well, Blincoe smiled and said, "I *have* to like them, by law," which should have been a tipoff to the crowd but probably didn't register with the neophytes in the group.

Lazovich turned out to be a bore. A stolid-looking, heavy-set man in a purple suit so garish that it made me want to stick a quarter in his mouth to see if he'd light up and play us a tune, he came across as a humorless, pompous selector of obvious favorites and dealt in such truisms about his choices as, "If they run good, I have money in my pocket. If they don't, I'm busted." Judging by his selections that morning, he must be busted a good deal of the time.

The only bright spot at this affair turned out to be Mary Bacon. Her choices to win races turned out to be no more accurate than those of Blincoe and Lazovich, but she made it clear that she entertained plenty of healthy doubts about horses with whose personal quirks she was unfamiliar and she was quick to explain why. "I like the five horse in this race," she said of one selection, for instance, "but he has the outside post at a mile and it may hurt him. In some of his races he seems to have a good closing move, but he'll

have to tuck in on the first turn and come through a hole
or he'll wind up in the parking lot. All horses will run outside of a horse, but some won't run inside." This was useful
talk for horseplayers and should have taught the less expe-
rienced something about the various ways horses can fail
to perform in a race.

Later, when taking questions from the floor, Mary
turned out to be equally adept. She talked freely about her
background, defined riding in quarter horse races as
"mostly just bootin' and scootin'" and reassured the women
in the audience that she had come to Del Mar to ride, not
to steal their husbands. "A lot of the owners' wives object
to me," she said, revealing that she was still finding it a
little difficult to get mounts, "but they ought to be worry-
ing about the go-go dancers in the bars their husbands stop
in on their way home." She looked very feminine and adorable in a low-cut, tight-fitting, short-sleeved dress and
open-toed shoes and, in fact, too delicately built to ride
race horses, but when challenged on this point she smiled,
held up her bare right arm and flexed an awesome bicep.
"Anyhow," she explained, "it's always a horse race, not a
jockey race."

The very next day, Mary Bacon won a race. Trainer
Henry Moreno put her up on the worst horse in his barn,
a South American plodder named Cumpa, who had never
even finished in the money in this country. Mary cut
through between horses with him on the turn for home, hit
him at least a couple of dozen times down the stretch to
keep him going and brought him in, at a delicious twenty-
three to one. She rode back to the winner's circle grinning

and was roundly cheered when she dismounted. I decided to get to know her a little better.

I found her early one morning around Eddie Goldstone's barn. Goldstone, a young ex-talent agent who is a relative newcomer to racing, was the only trainer then giving her mounts regularly, but he had only a small string of very mediocre horses, like Silver Salute, and she had been unable to win for him. The word around the backside was that Goldstone's interest in her was based on more than her riding skills, but I considered that irrelevant to what I wanted to find out about her. During the break we sat in Goldstone's tack room and chatted.

I quickly discovered that she wouldn't talk much about her childhood. I gathered, however, there was a father back there someplace in her past who had let her down. She gave the impression that she began hanging around horses as an escape. She grew up in New Mexico and Oklahoma and Texas and rode her first races when she was nine, at half-mile tracks in dusty little towns where they rode right down to the bone and nobody cared how old you were or what sex you were and people bet on the races with each other and not by ramming the money through a computerized machine. She'd ridden Thoroughbreds, quarter horses, Appaloosas, Indian ponies, just about anything that neighs and has four legs. "It don't matter what I ride," she said. "I can ride them as fast as they can run."

She'd fallen off quite a bit, too. She's broken her back twice, her pelvis once; she's cracked ribs and punctured a lung and fought off blood clots. It hadn't scared her or scarred her, but she had, I thought, the oldest-looking eyes I'd ever seen on a woman still in her twenties. She was married at fifteen to a sixteen-year-old jockey named Johnny Bacon, had a daughter by him, then went her own way again. The separation was very amicable, she claimed, but she received no alimony or child support, so she and little Susan and her mother now trailed together from track to track "so we can kind of help each other." Beyond the open door of the tack room, I could see Susan, small and as blond as her mother, playing among some bales of hay. Mary saw me looking at her and said, "I hope she's going to be a nun. That's safe, anyway."

She wasn't dating much, she told me, mostly because she didn't have the time. By six every morning she was at the track, galloping or working horses for Goldstone, Moreno, and anyone else who'd use her. "No trainer's going to put you up on his good horses in the afternoon if you can't get your ass out of bed to exercise them in the morning," she explained. At whatever hour, Mary looked terrific, I thought. She favored little polka-dot or flowered panties that showed up adorably through her riding silks. There are a lot of pretty girls around the stable area these days, but Mary Bacon was almost in a class by herself. "Boy, if you can ride as good as you look," I remembered one man calling to her in the paddock on opening day, "you can't lose, honey."

Mary Bacon's whole life had become the track. She'd go out more, she admitted, but had a realistic view of her situation. "Maybe if I was just some little bar-hopping chick, I'd do better," she said, "but, like one guy told me, I'm a divorcée with a six-year-old crumb snatcher." She got letters, though, a half-dozen or more a day, from men who'd like to meet her or dance with her "real close and slow." One faithful correspondent always signed himself "The Beast." Mary read all these letters but never answered them. The track was her world, the only one she wanted right then.

Above all, though, she wanted live mounts to ride. She knew she was being given only the pigs, but hoped that would change. Trainers are a conservative breed of men who don't like to risk their good horses with unknowns. What Mary and I didn't realize the morning we talked was that Cumpa would be her only winner of the meet, though I cashed place and show tickets on her at fancy prices during the following weeks. Mary's mounts were always overlays on the board, because the men at the track, who form the great majority of bettors, never expected her to do well at any price. But then Mary Bacon knew that and told me she wasn't out to prove anything to anyone anymore. She knew her own worth and simply hoped the men who dominate her chosen profession would come around.

I doubted that they would. I happened to be up in the press box on the day Mary brought Cumpa in. The general consensus up there was that the other riders had thrown her the race. "Hey, what does Cumpa mean?" somebody had shouted.

"It means cunt in Spanish," someone answered, but then the level of wit in the press box has never been high.

12

Getting Killed

The big black man was standing right down by the finish line and looking back toward the starting gate, where the horses for the ninth and final race of the day were about to be loaded into their stalls. The contest was at a mile and a sixteenth and involved the worst claiming horses on the grounds, the sort of event my friend Sam the Cynic once defined as "The Hospital Handicap," because so many of the animals involved are suffering from various crippling ailments. Ordinarily it is the sort of race one should never bet, except, perhaps, to risk a couple of dollars on a long-shot, but to the big black man it evidently represented his last chance to get even. He had a tattered *Form* sticking out of his back pocket, a fistful of ten-dollar win tickets in his left hand, and a giant pair of battered binoculars glued to his eyeballs. And he was talking loudly to himself. "Oh, Lord," he was saying, "now please just let him break good, oh, Lord! Don't let him get stuck in the gate, oh, Lord! Oh, sweet Lord, just get him out of there! I need this one, Lord! Have mercy, oh, Lord . . ."

When the gate opened and the horses came charging past him heading for the clubhouse turn, the big man kept right on invoking assistance in his time of trial. "Now, Lord," he said, "that was good! Now please don't let him get fanned on the turn! No, no, Lord, just keep him tucked in along the rail there, Lord, where he don't have to run too much too early! Oh, that's nice, Lord! Just like that! Oh, thank you, Lord!"

The field made the first turn and began its run down the backstretch. "Now, Lord," the big man continued, "just don't let him run yet, but don't let him get too far behind! We want him about five or six lengths off the leaders, Lord, and an honest pace up front! Oh, that's good, Lord, just like that! The half in forty-six and two, oh, that's nice, Lord, just about right! Just fast enough to cook that speed up front, Lord! Thank you, Lord! Now, Lord, when they hit the turn, let him make his move at about the three-eighths pole! Yes, Lord, but not too soon and don't let him get pocketed! We want him to run, oh, Lord! Yes, sir, to make that one big move of his, Lord!"

The horses began the turn for home. "Now, Lord, move him *now!*" the big man shouted. "Yeah, let him *roll,* Lord!" The horse the big man had been exorting his God to favor, a longshot who had been in the pack behind the front-runners, now did indeed begin to make his run, still tucked in along the rail. "That's it, Lord!" the big man shouted. "That's it! Now, Lord, now! Only don't let him get shut off, oh, Lord! Let that hole open up, Lord, and let him through! Glory be, Lord, just let him come home to me, Lord!"

As the field hit the head of the stretch, the big man's horse did get through on the rail and, with a burst of speed, exploded into the lead. An eighth of a mile from home, he was in front and pulling away, almost certainly a winner. The big black man glanced up at the sky and shook his binoculars at the clouds. "Oh, thank you, Lord, thank you! I got him now, Lord!" He glanced back at the track, where his choice continued to widen his margin as he rolled toward the finish line. "Yes, Lord, I got him now! Praise be the Lord!" the big man shouted, then saw his horse begin to shorten stride. *"Come o-o-on, you mother-fucker!"* he screamed. *"Stay up there, goddamn your eyes!"*

It occurred to me well into the meet that I stood a very real chance of getting killed here. Figuratively, of course, but in the pocketbook, where it can really hurt. During Hollywood Park I had been on a hot streak and ended up winning a total of about twenty-seven hundred dollars, no mean sum, considering that I rarely bet more than twenty dollars on any race and usually only five or ten. I had come to Del Mar fully aware of the pitfalls possibly await-ing me here and I began by betting cautiously, determined not to be annihilated and reminding myself constantly that I had endured the longest losing streak of my life at this track. But I had been lulled into a dangerous false sense of security. I won nearly three hundred dollars the first week, lost some of it back, then brought in a big Exacta early in the second week to go ahead by nearly four hun-dred dollars. Since then, however, I had been losing stead-

ily—twenty, thirty, sixty bucks at a clip—and one morning
I woke up to find myself down about three hundred. So
I did what I always do when I lose my touch at the track; I
went into my shell. I cut my bets in half, began to pass
more races and waited for the luck to turn.

By the end of the third week, I began to think my luck
might not turn at all. I was betting intelligently, I thought,
but the horses were running peculiarly. Let's consider one
typical day, a Friday. I began by backing an even-money
filly in the first race that figured to romp in by ten, but the
winner was an eleven to one shot my horse had slaugh-
tered in several previous meetings. I passed the second
race, won by another odds-on favorite I hadn't liked as
well as the one in the first. In the third, still another heavy
favorite came in, backed down to four to five. My wager
on this horse got me not quite even for the day. I then bet
twenty dollars on an animal I really liked in the fourth, at
two to one, only to watch him get left in the gate and
finish out of the money. In the fifth, I dropped another ten
dollars on a three-year-old chestnut filly named Swamp
Nurse, off at eight to one, ridden by a seventeen-year-old
apprentice rider who had evidently not yet learned how to
negotiate turns; Swamp Nurse tried to come eight wide
around the field and finished fourth. My selection in the
sixth came in second to a twelve to one shot I had given
absolutely no chance to and which won, leading all the
way, in a minute and fourteen seconds flat for the six furlongs, the slowest time ever here for a race at the distance
on a fast track. This statistic caused some hilarity in the
press box, but not from me.

I had three races left in which to try and get even. My

selection in the seventh, aptly named Incredibly and ridden by Donald Pierce, clipped the heels of a horse in front
of her and went down, sending poor Pierce tumbling into
the dirt. Luckily he wasn't hurt, but the mishap wreaked
further havoc on my wallet. In the eighth, my choice ran
third and in the ninth I was beaten, at eight to one on a
Shoemaker mount, by a horse that had lost its seventeen
previous starts and never figured to have any chance at all.
My net loss for the day was eighty-three dollars, but it
might as well have been a thousand to judge by the rotten
taste I had at the back of my throat. There is nothing quite
so galling to a horseplayer as the conviction that he is losing for no particular reason that he can understand. It's
enough to make a man believe in voodoo or to ascribe his
bad fortunes to a sinister cabal of enemies in league to
break him. I walked out of the track that day feeling like
an idiot, both for blowing so much money again and for
not knowing what I was doing wrong.

The one major consolation on any losing streak is that
there are always people worse off than you are. On my way
out of the track that afternoon, I found myself briefly in
step with Tommy, a black businessman and investor better
known to me and others as Tap-Out. He looked white,
which isn't easy for him because his normal color is ebony.
He informed me that he had won the first four races, including the Daily Double, to get about five thousand to
the good, but had blown it all back plus another five grand
by the end of the day. I commiserated with him, though I
must now shamefully acknowledge that I immediately
began to feel a lot better about my own developing disaster. Dropping five thousand at the track in a single day

is not as serious a matter to Tap-Out as dropping a couple of hundred would be to me, but it's the sort of statistic that makes me feel a shade less idiotic.

What I'm talking about here is ego gratification, because, after the vigorish has been peeled away from your bets, picking winners and making money at the track is a form of competition, a ruthless contest of skills between you and everyone else there, since the odds on every horse are ultimately established solely by the amount of money wagered on his nose. A bad losing streak means not only financial depletion, but testifies painfully and irrefutably to the unwelcome reality that a lot of other people are winning money at your expense. A long losing streak can shrivel the scrotum and atrophy the testicles. It's no accident that most heavy gamblers are men; two-fisted bettors are, among other things, asserting their manhood, even if in the silliest way imaginable.

I got to thinking, after my encounter with Tap-Out, that probably the best way to put an end to my losing streak would be to find some big plunger and simply go against his action. There are days when Tap-Out, for instance, will sweep the card and leave the premises with a bankroll the size of a small duffle bag, but they are very far between; most of the time he gets killed. The fashionable theory about his kind is that, for reasons rooted in their subconscious, they want to lose, they want to punish themselves. I'm not going to debate this point at length, mainly because it doesn't interest or convince me. There are, of course, hooked gamblers, betting junkies of all sorts, but there are also a lot of types, like Tap-Out, who are out there not so much to lose (he's a winner at his career, for

one thing) as to prove their superiority, at least to themselves, by knocking over the house or beating some other
cat out of his loot. *Machismo* is as much in evidence at the
track as elsewhere, as any reading of Ernest Hemingway's
romanticized accounts of his own exploits at the races will
attest to, but *machismo* is only one element in a larger
emotion.

I, too, know the feeling well, because, after an especially
good day, I am utterly and totally relaxed, not only a
demon in bed, but the master of my fate, the captain of
my soul, and the one human being upon whom and in
whom all knowledge, wisdom, and understanding rest. It
has nothing to do with winning money (I despise most
forms of gambling, loathe Las Vegas, and hardly ever bet
on horses with bookies), but has everything to do with the
rapture that comes from having, temporarily at least,
touched upon an answer to one of the most mystifying
riddles of the universe, the puzzle of what makes one person a winner in life and another a loser. Solve that one and
immortality awaits you. In fact, I thought to myself after
saying goodbye to Tap-Out that if I could solve Del Mar,
I might qualify, if not for true immortality, at least for in-
stant nirvana. Beating this meet was becoming a labor
beside which those of Hercules seemed trifling.

If only I could have located Vince Edwards. Of all the
celebrities I know who frequent the track, from Fred
Astaire to Mickey Rooney to Walter Matthau, Jack Klugman, and Telly Savalas, Edwards, the surly looking star of
a *schlock* television series and several indifferent movies,
is surely one of the biggest and most consistently wrong-
headed of bettors. I've seen him chuck it in through the

fifty and hundred-dollar windows on horses with no more chance to win the race than a lame goat and I have never, ever, seen him cash a ticket, though, of course, he must from time to time. Everyone, by the law of averages, must bring in a winner every now and then, but Vince Edwards must surely bring in fewer than anyone else. Furthermore, he has a hangdog look about him at the track, as if he knows that the deck is stacked against him and fate is sure to be merciless in its persistent humiliation of him. I once got myself out of a bad losing day at Santa Anita by over-hearing him aggressively sound the virtues of a horse in the last race that I also happened to have bet on. I rushed back to the window, sold my ticket, and bet another horse, a ten to one longshot that promptly came romping in an easy winner. Edwards' choice proceeded to break down at the quarter pole and had to be carted off the track in a meat wagon. Vince Edwards, I decided on my ride back to the motel, might be the solution now, but I hadn't yet seen him at Del Mar. He might be working somewhere and out of reach. The trouble with actors is you can't count on them.

I could, of course, have opted to spend all my time in the press box, which houses a small mob of dedicated losers, but I ultimately decided against it. There's so much talk up there and so much misinformation bandied about that it's distracting to a serious handicapper, nor is there anyone to compare to such glorious plungers as Tap-Out. Besides, wandering about among the regulars is really the only entertaining way to go racing. At Santa Anita, for example, I often share a box with three people I've come to be very fond of: Sena Deats, a handsome, older lady of some means, who is always elegantly dressed and unfailingly gracious; Gloria Carroll, an attractive, dark-haired woman with a ready laugh, who supports herself as a waitress in a local restaurant; and Jack Glass, a middle-aged plumbing wholesaler from Arcadia, who has an elfish sense of humor and a small but insistent penchant for mild *doubles entendres* and dreadful puns. The four of us see each other only at the track and have, I suspect, little in common away from it, but we are indissolubly united by our one incurable addiction. I wouldn't trade their company at the races for that of any so-called expert or, for instance, any of the large gaggle of snobs who never stir from their cushy seats in the Turf Club. Going to the races is not just betting money on horses; it's also spending time with some good people. My problem at Del Mar was not only my inability to win with any regularity, but was being compounded, I realized, by not having any of my best cronies on hand with whom to commiserate.

I tried Barry Irwin. He and a young trainer named Tom Bunn, with whom he shared a room, were perched at one end of the bar at the Lodge this particular night and I joined them. Barry, who doesn't drink because he's convinced himself that alcohol destroys the brain cells and someday he's going to get back to his novel with all of his faculties unimpaired, was well into his second ginger ale. Furthermore, he was having plenty of troubles of his own—with a soon-to-be ex-wife, a current girl friend, his editors and the proofreaders at the *Form*, as well as a choice selection of mortal locks that had refused to behave obligingly for him of late—so many troubles, in fact, that I discovered he didn't have time to hear any of mine. So I turned to Bunn, a tall, gangly Californian with the slightly dazed look of a man two or three years behind in his sleep and who, to judge by the healthily dark-brown color of the liquid in his glass, harbored no silly reservations about the possible rape of his brain cells by the great demon alcohol. "I didn't know you were staying in this whorehouse," were his first words to me. "Let's get the hell out of here and drink in some decent place." The last thing he wanted to do, it turned out, was talk horses. "Horses?" he said. "Horses? Shit, I got a barn full of horses so bad they can't even finish the races I enter them in. And every day, practically, I have to call my owners and tell them sad stories. One thing we are not going to do tonight is talk about horses."

We spent most of the night, of course, talking about horses and, especially, about the funny goings-on at Del Mar. There was the race, for instance, in which jockey Paco Mena got an X rating. Up on a two-year-old maiden filly named Leal's Jewel, Mena went for the lead at the head of the stretch, but his mount, according to the chart in the *Form* the next day, "faltered along the rail while the jock's pants came apart." I had bet the winner in that race, but the event simply served to prove that there are countless ways to lose at the track. Recently, at Hollywood Park, I had backed a mare trained by Bobby Frankel that, no more than twenty yards from home and two lengths in front, had bolted and left the course, taking part of the inside railing with her. "Every time you think you've seen everything at the track," Barry said, "something will happen that you've never seen before, and usually to your disadvantage."

"How about the boat races they have here?" a man standing next to us said. "I never seen so many at one meet. They're running one a day."

"The jockeys need a better pension plan," Bunn mused.

"Are you implying that some of the races here are fixed?" Barry asked, in mock dismay.

"Not fixed, exactly," the stranger said, "but in some of them they should maybe equip the riders with canoe paddles instead of whips, so the public would know in advance and then it would simply become a question of guessing whose turn it was."

"They could call the thing a regatta in the program," Bunn suggested. "That would be one way."

"What specific race are you referring to?" Barry asked.

The stranger, a thin type with a day's growth of dark beard and the look of a man who had just drunk a pint of pure vinegar, now cited the example of a recent contest in which a once famous jockey had come out of retirement after a couple of years, having been unable to make it in the business world. His mount in a short field had been trapped behind a wall of horses on the turn for home, but all the leaders had obligingly swung wide to let him through at the head of the stretch and he'd won his comeback going away. It was the only race he was to win at the whole meet.

"Well," Bunn said, "that was more of a benefit."

"Yes," I agreed, "especially for the people who guessed correctly and cashed tickets."

"There's a lot of shit going on here," the stranger said, "but I don't ever read anything about it in the *Form*." He looked at Barry. "How come you guys write nothing about it?"

Barry shrugged, but I knew why. The *Racing Form* has no competition. Its handicappers, clockers, statisticians, and reporters receive the full cooperation of the racing establishment at every meet all over the country and it is not about to jeopardize its privileged position by rocking the boat even slightly.

The success of racing depends almost entirely upon the confidence of the public that the proceedings are as honest as possible and conducted under the strict supervision of officials whose integrity is beyond question. The fact of the matter is, however, that many races are not honest, in the strictest sense of the word. Horses are still doped ("medicated" is the euphemism the establishment prefers); jockeys still carve up races between them, especially those involving Exacta payoffs and other forms of combination wagers; trainers still enter horses in races wtih no intention of trying to win them, either because the animals aren't ready but need the exercise and experience or because they're trying to get the odds up high enough to cash tickets on them at a later date, a tactic much talked about around the track but never mentioned publicly by people officially connected to racing; crippled or ailing animals on the verge of breaking down and obviously too sore to run appear on the track every day of every meet and are only very rarely not permitted to compete by the track veterinarians, who are empowered to scratch them even at the last second and clearly should do so; and a great many infrac-

tions committed during the running of the races themselves
are ignored by the stewards, whose job it is to ensure that
every horse in a race runs without interfering with any
other horse, either intentionally or by accident.

The basic reason that all of these things still occur and
will continue to occur is that racing polices itself. It ap-
points most of its own officials, all of whom are culled
from the ranks and are totally dependent on racing for
their livelihood (many of them are ex-jockeys and ex-
trainers), while those selected by the state and supposedly
representing the interests of the general public are inevitably political appointees, who are not about to jeopardize either their cushy sinecures or the steady flow of
money into government coffers.

This overall situation persists and is made possible by
the indifference of the daily press to racing, which ranks
low in the estimation of most editors. The racing writers
rarely stir from the press box, where they receive free food
and drink, can watch other sports events or old movies on
TV between races, and turn out copy based mostly on
handouts provided by the track publicity department or
group interviews set up by these obliging folk. Most racing columnists are not even writers and their editors have
no interest in making them do any investigative reporting;
they are, with a few exceptions, purely and simply horseplayers who have found an easy way to support their habit.
The only writer I saw regularly in the stable area during
the Del Mar meeting was Irwin, whose attempts to write
honestly about what he saw were too often frustrated by
his editors. It would be expecting too much of the people

at the *Form*, I suppose, to take any risks, since the racing associations and tracks could, without too much trouble, publish their own racing statistics and include them in every program, but then we live in a country that was supposedly founded by risk-takers. If, as I suspect, nothing will ever be done to correct these abuses, then the very least we could ask on behalf of the public is that the same criteria be applied to racing as to the smoking of cigarettes. I'd like to see a box clearly stamped on every program that explains exactly what it costs to make a bet and a warning that playing the horses could be hazardous to the health of your bank account. All right, I know I'm a dreamer.

When I communicated some of the above thoughts to my drinking companions, they laughed. "It will never happen," Bunn said. "How's everyone going to make a living?"

"Listen," Barry whispered, "I'll tell you something *really* important, Whittingham has a horse going tomorrow you can bet your *tochas* on . . ."

The point of all this, really, is that horseplayers are incurable. They would go to the races no matter what the odds against them or the circumstances. And I am no exception.

On December 7, 1941, two friends named Arnie and Dale met during the course of the day at Caliente, then the only track on the continent conducting Sunday racing. Dale was late getting to the track and had been listening to the radio on the drive down from San Diego. He came rushing into the grandstand area and spotted Arnie, already deep into his study of the *Form*. "Hey, Arnie," Dale

shouted as he ran up to him, "did you hear?"
"Hear what?"
"The Japanese just bombed Pearl Harbor!"
"Yeah?" Arnie said. "Who do you like in the fourth?"

13

Looking for the Wonder Sucker

"You seem like a sensible guy and I like to hear you talk about everything except racing," the man I'm going to call Ivan Casey said to me. "About horses you got a head full of Chinese rice."

"I wasn't talking about horses," I said. "I was talking about trainers."

"No difference," Ivan Casey said. "You people on the outside just don't know what you're talking about."

I wasn't having a good night. We were still about two-thirds of the way through the meet and I was still losing, not much now, but steadily. Furthermore, the funny things that had been happening to me every day no longer amused me at all. I had been misinformed twice in the same morning by trainers I had respected, had spent a wretched afternoon watching their assessments of their animals' chances prove to be totally unfounded and I had come wandering into the bar of the Lodge looking for

booze and companionable ears to sound off to. Barry, Pat
Rogerson, and this man Casey, whom I didn't know, had
been sitting at a table together and I had joined them. We
had been getting into it ever since.

To begin with, Rogerson was battling demons of his
own and was in a foul temper, which he took out initially
on the waitress. Barry, who doesn't enjoy scenes, quickly
departed. I had begun to talk about the trouble with trainers, only to discover that Casey was himself a trainer and at
that particular moment not inclined to be either tolerant
of my assessment of the species or sympathetic to my woes.
He had woes of his own. He had no clients, no horses, and
a young wife with a new baby on his hands.

He was firm but even-tempered with me, I have to grant
him that. His main point seemed to be that most trainers
were honest, hard-working souls who were completely
misunderstood and were being constantly second-guessed
by their clients, the owners. "I try very hard," he said. "I
do the best I can, but the owners don't leave you alone.
They're always sticking their noses in and fouling things
up."

"Why shouldn't they?" I said. "They're paying the bills.
In what other business would an owner simply turn over
his property and be expected to disappear?"

Casey shrugged off the point, because, according to him,
racing wasn't like any other human activity. Only the
trainer spent any time with the animals and he was the
only one qualified to make decisions. "I'd do OK, if they'd
leave me alone, but I get nothing but trouble from
owners," he said and added that he'd come to Del Mar
hoping to pick up some horses and get back in action. "I've

never had a good owner, never," he concluded. "I know
I could do a good job, if I was left alone to do it."

I decided that my timing had been atrocious, so I allowed the discussion to lapse. After all, here was a man in
his late thirties, out of work and with a wife and child to
support, and I was knocking his profession. It wouldn't
have been exactly classy of me to belabor the argument, so
I accepted his somewhat humiliating estimate of my own
knowledge in the field and kept my usually voluble mouth
shut.

Later, however, at Bully's, a superactive drinking and
social center in the town of Del Mar, I ran into my friend
Gary, the volleyball enthusiast, and asked him about
Casey. I recollected having seen his name from time to
time on racing programs, but I couldn't recall what horses
he'd ever trained.

"Casey?" Gary said. "He's not a trainer. He's a handicapper who got himself a trainer's license. He knows even
less about horses than most trainers."

"How'd he get his license?"

"Don't ask me," Gary said, "but unless you're Jewish or
Mexican or black, all they ask you is about five questions.
Casey's like most of these guys; they're all dreaming of the
wonder sucker, some rich dummy who'll come along with
a fat blank check and let them do what they want. There
are plenty of wonder suckers around, too, only Casey's
too dumb to have nailed one."

"You don't think there's any merit to what he says?"

"Why don't you just ask him why he doesn't put his own
money on the line?" Gary said. "I mean, if he's so goddam
talented, why doesn't he raise a little money—it wouldn't

be hard for him—and go and claim some horses of his own? None of these guys like Casey will ever shoot craps with their own money."

By the time I showed up in the backside just before seven one morning, with the sky a dull gray overhead and a cold, misty wind coming in off the sea, George Williams had already been up a couple of hours. During the Del Mar meet every year, he lives alone in a nearby motel and drives back and forth to the track, where this season his small string of horses was stabled in Barn H-H, a good location because of its easy access to the gap through which the horses go out to work or gallop in the morning. Williams is not fond of Del Mar, primarily because it takes him a bit too far from his home base in L.A., where his wife runs a dress shop and his young son goes to school. But he also dislikes it because the early-morning climate is chilly and damp, not kind to a slightly built, very lean ex-rider of forty-eight who is always short of sleep.

He was taking a break when I caught up to him, his feet propped up on the battered desk in his tack room, a soiled white-canvas tennis hat jammed down on his head and a plastic cup full of hot, watery track-kitchen coffee in his hand. He didn't look at all well. Williams has gray hair, light-blue eyes, and the normally ruddy complexion of his native Ireland, where he was born and lived until he moved to the states about twenty-five years ago. This particular morning, however, his face was flushed and his eyes were watery. He looked, in fact, like a man with a very bad cold, who was clearly running a temperature and should never have gotten out of bed at all. "I get this every year at Del Mar," he said. "It's the weather down here. Too damp." He made it clear that there was nothing to be done about it; he didn't run a huge public stable with competent assistants who could oversee things in his absence and you couldn't just not show up when there was work to be done. Horses need a lot of looking after.

While he finished his coffee, Williams gave me a quick rundown on his current situation. He worked mainly for one owner, the Bullwinkle Stable of Jay Ward, creator of the comical moose and the other cartoon characters who cavort daily across the nation's TV screens, but in addition he also had a couple of nags for other people. At the moment his string at Del Mar consisted of eight, including two of Bullwinkle's best, the stakes-winning horses Chief Hawk Ear and Chief Pronto, both of them difficult and trouble-prone animals who required more than the normal amount of care. Chief Hawk Ear, a particularly capable performer on grass, was so fragile that Williams considered himself lucky to get four or five races a year out of him and Chief Pronto was always coming down with some small ailment or other or getting himself messed up in races. "Every horse eventually breaks down," Williams explained. "The main thing is not to get too attached to them. You try to keep them sound as long as you can, at least long enough to win some money with them." He added that he had just about given up any hope of running Chief Hawk Ear at Del Mar, because the turf course, after nearly a month of racing, had been chopped to pieces and was full of rough spots and holes, too risky going for the stable's top performer. "But even the main track is pretty bad," he said. "You see, all tracks are OK the first weeks of a meeting, then the surface bunches up and that's when the horses really begin to break down."

I stood outside the shed row for about twenty minutes and watched Williams supervise the labors of his four grooms, all of whom had been working steadily for hours mucking out stalls, forking in fresh straw and hay, curry-combing and sponging and cooling out horses. One groom, a tall, sad-eyed Puerto Rican, spent most of the morning walking endlessly in circles with one or another of the stable's horses. It takes about an hour to cool out a horse after a workout and Williams won't use the spidery-looking, electrically powered machines that have become a common sight in the stable areas. "We hand hot-walk all my horses," he explained. "I used those damn machines, even though I never liked them, until I had three horses get tangled up in them. That filly running today has a scar on her neck from it and she's lucky she's alive and racing, though I don't know how lucky *we* are."

The filly he referred to was aptly named Lucky Coloul-lah, a three-year-old chestnut of some ability but nervous habits. She was entered in the fifth race that day, at a mile, and would go off as one of the longshots. "She could win it," Williams commented. "It just depends how she behaves before the race." At the moment she was standing quietly in her stall and I walked over to scratch her nose and pat her neck, where the scar, a deep indentation, from her tiff with the machine was clearly visible. "Come on," Williams said, after a minute or two, "I have to go enter a horse for next Monday. Then I've got to get back here in time for the boy to gallop Chief Pronto. He's not easy to ride and I have to talk to him."

We walked over to the racing office, where he wrote the name of the Monday horse, Clank, on an entry blank and handed it in. At the time he did so, with only about half an hour before the entries closed, there were only three other horses so far committed to the race, which meant that, unless at least two more showed up, it wouldn't be run at all and would be replaced on the Monday card by another one with conditions designed to attract a larger field. "I hope it goes," Williams said, as we headed back toward his barn. "I think he'll win easily." Clank, he explained, had once been potentially a really good horse, but had broken down and had had to be brought back very slowly, after many months of rest and care. He never did live up to the hopes everyone had for him, but he could win races against the cheaper claiming horses going over a distance of ground. The race on Monday was at a mile and a quarter, ideal for him. "He usually goes to the front, but he can come from off as well," Williams said. "I like him on the front end. He runs with his tail flashing and the riders behind him think he's really flying and will tire, but he's just going easy. Shoemaker rides him perfectly, because he knows him and he's the best judge of pace there is. He'll never ask a horse to use himself up too early."

When we got back to Barn II-II, jockey Steve Valdez's agent, a good-looking, soft-spoken young guy with a thick head of tightly curled blond hair, was waiting for him, on the off-chance that Williams might have a mount for his client. The trainer was affable enough but offered no tangible encouragement, so the agent left quickly to make more rounds, a crumpled condition book sticking out of the rear pocket of his jeans. Valdez had once been a popular rider, but, like so many others after losing their bugs, he'd since drifted into obscurity. Lately, though, he'd been winning some races again and was getting up on some live mounts, but not from Williams. "I'd put Shoe on *all* my horses, if I could," he said. "You don't have to tell him anything. If he doesn't know what to do on a horse, nothing you can tell him is going to help much." Of course, Williams made it clear, Shoe is so much in demand it's hard to get him, especially as the bigger, richer stables tend to have prior call on his services. "Also, he doesn't like to ride too many races down here, because it's sort of a vacation for him," he said. "He rides for Whittingham, of course, and in all the big races. But I hope I can get him up on Clank, if this one fills. He's won with him before." Lucky Coloullah, I had noticed, would be ridden by Fernando Toro, not a bad second choice, as he was leading the rider standings at the moment. Shoe was scheduled to ride Swamp Nurse, the probable favorite.

The exercise boy who'd been hired to gallop Chief Pronto failed to show up on schedule and Williams decided to take him out himself. Ordinarily he gallops his own horses a good deal of the time, but Chief Pronto, a small horse with a big temper and a lot of nasty habits, struck me as too tough a customer for a middle-aged man with a temperature and badly clogged sinuses. "He bites, you know, and about once a week he props and I wind up in the dirt," the trainer confided, as one of his grooms, grinning hugely, gave him a leg up onto Chief Pronto's back. "I think I'm making a big mistake." We set off for the track, though I was careful to stay well out of range of Chief Pronto's hooves. Thoroughbreds can be as mean as they are stupid and I reasoned that a horse who would bite and throw his trainer would think nothing of flattening a total stranger.

Just as Williams and Chief Pronto reached the gap, a horse came galloping past going the wrong way in the middle of the track. The boy riding him, white-faced with fear, was standing straight up in the stirrups and pulling as hard as he could on the reins, but the saddle had slipped and the animal was obviously out of control. Voices shouted warnings from the track and guinea stand, while two outriders on their fast ponies took off in pursuit. Luckily, after no more than a few seconds, one of the outriders caught up to the runaway, leaned over to catch his bridle and brought him under control. An audible murmur of relief could be heard from the watchers, including myself, in the stands. Several years ago I'd been present when a fast maiden two-year-old had thrown his rider during a workout and had come hurtling back along the inside rail in the wrong direction. He'd collided at full speed with two horses working in tandem and all three animals had been killed, though, miraculously, none of the riders had been badly hurt. "You may be an atheist before and after you've been involved in one of these," Williams commented later, "but during one, if it's you up there on the horse's back, you pray to God good and hard."

Luckily for Williams, Chief Pronto turned out to be on his best behavior this morning and the trainer managed to gallop him around the track once without falling off, though his thin, gaunt face was beet-red from the exertion. "Sometimes I know I'm in the wrong business," he said, as he started back to the barn.

After making sure nothing else needed his urgent attention, Williams and I hurried once more to the racing office,
where the trainer heard that Clank's race had drawn three
more entries and would be run as scheduled. "Now I've got
to call the owner," he said and proceeded to explain that
Clank actually had several owners, all but one of whom
took little interest in the horse's fortunes. They'd originally
bought him on Williams' recommendation, expecting to
have invested in a good allowance or stakes competitor, and
had lost interest in him once he'd hurt himself and wound
up as a cheap plater. "This man is the only one in the
group who cares at all," Williams said, stepping into one of
the phone booths outside the racing office. "I always keep
him informed, because, if he can, he likes to fly down here
from Oregon to see him run." He dialed, pumped a fistful
of change into the machine, and waited for his owner to
pick up the phone. "Hello, Mr. Wright? It looks like we're
in business."

By the time we got back to the barn again, the sun had
begun to burn off the fog and the rest of the day gave
promise of becoming a good one, but not for Williams.
The first item he heard was that one of his grooms had
found heat in Chief Pronto's left front hoof, indicating the
probability of an infection of some kind. The trainer went
to work treating it himself, while I walked down his shed
row to take a look at Chief Duffy, "a maiden who's going
to be a good one," I'd been told. The young colt was
standing quietly at the back of his stall, but he looked like
a runner. His coat gleamed and his head had the noble,
indefinable look of a champion. "You can always tell a
good horse from a mediocre one," Williams had said ear-

lier. "They just look it. They know who they are." Duffy
was the sort of horse who wouldn't put out on the track
until some other animal decided to run with him, at which
point he'd dig in. He was a real competitor, which is absolutely the best quality a racehorse of whatever ability can
have. "I'd rather train a cheap cripple who'll give you all
he's got," Willis Reavis had once told me, "than one of
these suckers that burns up the track in the morning and
don't run a lick in the afternoon." (My morning with Williams eventually turned out to be profitable, because I remembered what he'd said about Chief Duffy and I bet him
when he debuted at Santa Anita two months later and won
by a nose, at twenty to one.)

Later, one of the track vets came by and also took a look
at Chief Pronto, then checked another ailing horse that
Williams was bringing up to a race through a series of ailments that included a torn shoulder muscle and a chron-
ically sore back. By eleven o'clock the trainer had already
put in a full-time working day and we parted at last as he
headed back to his motel to try and get a little rest before
he'd have to show up frontside for Lucky Coloullah's race.
I went home myself and slept until noon.

About twenty minutes after the fifth race that afternoon,
I dropped by the paddock to see what Williams was up to
and found him, still wheezy and flushed, all dressed up in a
jacket and tie. He also looked more than mildly disgusted.
"Look at her," he said. "She's washing out." Lucky Coloullah was indeed a wreck. She was standing in her saddling
stall, quivering and bathed in sweat. Her owner Jay Ward,
a round, balding middle-aged man with a large walrus
mustache, stood by, seemingly unconcerned by this dis-

tressing spectacle. "She won't run much today," Williams said. Ward nodded, but indicated he'd put a few dollars on her anyway, a fact that did not surprise Williams because the owner bets all of his horses in every one of their races. "She'd be a nice filly," Williams said, "if I could just find a way to get her to settle down."

I sat directly behind Williams in the Bullwinkle box over the finish line and watched Lucky Coloullah show a brief burst of speed when she came out of the starting gate, then fade back to finish next to last, just ahead of one of Tom Bunn's barnful of bums. Shoemaker brought Swamp Nurse in second, which cost me some money, as I had picked her to win.

I walked down through the crowd toward the track with Williams and asked him what the immediate future held for him. "You go from day to day," he said, "depending on what comes up. It's hard to plan too far ahead in this business. Right now I'll make sure this filly came out of the race sound, then I'll go back to talk to Mr. Ward. Later I'll go over to the barn to make sure the horses are OK, then I'll grab some supper and go to bed. I'm usually through by ten o'clock."

"George," I said, "there must be an easier way to make a living."

"If there is and I find out about it," he answered, "I'm going to get real depressed."

About a week later I found myself standing next to Ivan Casey at the rail of the paddock as the horses in a cheap claiming race came walking into the ring. We nodded cautiously to each other, but before either of us could say anything Bobby Frankel came up on Casey's other side and the two men began to talk. I missed most of what Casey was saying, but it must have had something to do with his recent misfortunes. Frankel, who looks like an angry, overweight New York street kid and is not celebrated either for his modesty or his gracious manners, suddenly cut him off. "Your trouble is you don't deliver," he said. "You have to win races and you don't win. What do you expect?" Abruptly he turned and walked away. I studied my program very hard and pretended not to have overheard, though I don't think Casey was fooled. To this day, whenever we bump into each other around the track, he does his best to pretend he doesn't see me.

I reported the gist of this conversation to Barry Irwin, who's had his own troubles with Frankel when the trainer objects to items about himself that he considers unflattering in Barry's column. "You can't fault Frankel on winning races," Barry said. "I suppose that's what this is all about. You don't have to be a great human being to be a winner."

14

Maybe It Never Comes Back

Dan Smith was working in publicity for both Santa Anita and Del Mar in early 1973 when he heard a rumor that Johnny Longden was talking about making a comeback. Longden had retired in 1966 to become a successful trainer, after forty years as a rider and a total of six thousand and thirty-two winners, a record that stood until Bill Shoemaker broke it at Del Mar in 1970. But, the way Dan heard it, Longden still had this itch to race ride. He had a nice Round Table maiden colt in his barn named Circle that he'd been working himself in the mornings and he'd just about convinced himself that he was the boy to get on the horse for its debut. He was unable, however, to convince his wife Hazel and, by the time Dan got around to checking into the story, she'd wisely talked her husband out of it.

"It got me to thinking, though," Dan told me. "It occurred to me, lying in bed one night, that maybe jockeys, like old ballplayers, don't ever quite lose their hunger to stay in the game and we could bring a whole bunch of them out of retirement for just one race every year, sort of an equivalent to baseball's Old-Timers Game." He talked the idea over with Donald Smith (no relation), his boss at Del Mar, then went to Longden's son Vance and asked him if he thought his dad would ride in such a race. When Vance said he probably would, Dan knew he was in business. Within the next few weeks he'd lined up a representative field of old riders, including Longden himself, organized a race for them at five and a half furlongs on cheap claiming horses to be run during the Del Mar meet and began beating publicity drums right and left. The music sounded loud and clear, especially after Donald Smith came up with a catchy name for the event, the Rocking Chair Derby, and then went out and bought an old wooden rocker for the winning rider to sit in after the race and take custody of until the following year.

Longden didn't win the 1973 inaugural running, though he was briefly out in front on a cheap speedball named Merakos, and the experience retired him for keeps. The problem wtih putting on the Rocking Chair Derby every year, Dan Smith soon discovered, is that it's a lot tougher to ride in a single competitive race than to play three innings of slow-motion baseball. Though the Derby is essentially an exhibition, with no parimutuel wagering allowed, the purse is a real one and both trainers and owners would like to win it, or at least pick up some piece of it. Nor are the horses aware of any difference in the proceedings; they're out there to run, not gallop around the track with some old geezers bouncing happily up and down on their

backs while everybody cheers. The old-timers who ride in
the Rocking Chair have to be fit and ready and so they
train hard for it. And not for the thousand dollars they can
get paid for winning it or the five hundred they're guaranteed just for appearing in it either. "I'm riding in it because
I figure I owe it to the game and because it's fun," Ralph
Neves told reporters. "I'm getting old, you know. Getting
fit for this race is no joke. It's hard work and can spoil your
summer, if you like playing golf. But if I can get on a live
horse and have some fun, it'll be worth it." Neves, who was
fifty-three at the time, won three thousand seven hundred and seventy-one races during his career and retired
abruptly one morning in 1964, when he suddenly realized
on his way to the track that, after thirty years, "it just
wasn't fun anymore." It's amazing how nine years in the
restaurant business can bring the sense of fun back, or is it
simply that, as Neves also observed, "it's hard for any
athlete to admit that he's over the hill"?

The third running of the Derby, set for August 20, prom-
ised to be the best one yet. Dan Smith had lined up eight
riders, including the 1973 and 1974 winners, Dean Hall
and Ken Church. Neves was back for a third try and also
on hand were Dave Gorman, Bill Harmatz, George Taniguchi, and Angel Valenzuela, each of whom had earned
over four million dollars in purses during their careers. I
decided that the man I'd root for, however, was the eighth
contestant, Hubert Trent, participating for the first time at
the age of sixty-three. I knew nothing about Trent as a
rider, except that during his career, from 1942 to 1956, he'd
booted home nine hundred and eighteen winners, earned
his owners over two million dollars in purses and been the

subject of a briefly popular racetrack rhyme, "Pay the rent with Hubert Trent," probably coined by an ecstatic beneficiary of a triumph on some improbable longshot. Since then, for nearly twenty years, Trent had been working in the backside as an exercise boy, so completely forgotten by the racing establishment that he hadn't even been invited to participate in the first two runnings of the Rocking Chair. He'd won some big races, too, at Del Mar, including the La Jolla Handicap in 1946 and the inaugural of the Del Mar Futurity in 1948. Though Dan Smith had known about him, it had taken a feature story about him by Barry Irwin in the *Form* to remind everyone else of his presence on the grounds and his obvious eligibility. I intended to root for Trent, if only because he was ten years older than anyone else in the race and obviously "had more guts than a two-ton hog," according to one estimate of his prowess I overheard in the bar of the Lodge.

The drawing for horses and post positions took place early Sunday morning, three days before the race. By nine o'clock several hundred people were milling around the backside racing office, waiting for the Honorary Stewards to show up. Dan Smith had easily persuaded Longden and Johnny Adams, another celebrated ex-rider turned trainer, to serve and then pulled off a major publicity coup by importing Eddie Arcaro from his home in Miami.

Arcaro was the greatest rider I've ever seen, not only because he had talent to spare, but also because he was almost always trying. He was a canny judge of pace, a tremendous finisher, and absolutely fearless, despite the usual number of bad spills every rider takes during his career. In the immortal words of his first agent Nick Huff, inter-

viewed by the late A. J. Liebling when Arcaro was only
twenty-two and just coming into his own, "We are par ex-
cellence the best rider in the country, from one jump to
four miles." By the time I'd first become aware of Arcaro,
he'd established himself as "The Master," though to most
of us who used to bet on him, especially when the odds
were right, he was more affectionately known as "Old
Banana Nose," a tribute to the most prominent adornment
of his long Latin face. He'd retired a wealthy man in 1961,
had survived open-heart surgery, and had never been up
on a horse since. Unlike most other ex-wonders of the sporting world, he'd also turned out to have a charismatic
public presence, much in demand for a fee at banquets,
conventions, and such, and his presence at the Rocking
Chair Derby seemed destined to convert the event into a
media triumph. In fact, I'd already noticed that Dan Smith
had been generating a tremendous amount of publicity for
the affair, though the major networks had not yet made
a bid to televise the proceedings nationally. That would
come, maybe next year, Dan felt. Old Banana Nose would
see to that.

When Arcaro, looking trim and prosperous in a tailored
leisure suit, finally did show up, escorted by Dan Smith
and surrounded by *paparazzi* snapping pictures, the scene
outside the racing office became a joyful reunion. The old-
timers, who'd known him when, crowded around to shake
his hand and banter with him, while the younger men,
who'd only heard of him, formed a loosely grouped outer
circle of curious, slightly awed onlookers. Arcaro had a
word for everyone and established himself immediately as
the perfect emcee, fast on his feet and full of banter, with-

out ever losing that edge of sheer class that had enthralled me the first time I'd ever seen him boot a winner home. When the drawing finally got under way and Ken Church came up with a speedy horse called The Bureaucrat in the number five post position, Arcaro grinned and said, "Good, Kenny, now you can shut off the four guys inside of you."

"Not me, he can't," George Taniguchi said quickly. He was laughing harder than anyone else because he'd drawn on the outside, which is where you're least likely to get hurt in any race.

The only person during the morning who wasn't enjoying himself was Hector Palma, a tall, dark-haired, copper-skinned man who trained Wally Laub, one of the entries in the Derby. His horse had been drawn by Hubert Trent in the four hole and Palma clearly didn't think any sixty-three-year-old rider would be able to handle him; Wally Laub was a four-year-old gelding that had once had some class, but he was a headstrong, difficult animal to control. A jockey's agent, who happened to overhear Palma's pessimistic assessment of his chances, did his best to reassure him. "It's OK," he said. "The first guy out of the gate wins this race, because the others all take back." Palma shrugged, shook his head, and left.

After the drawing was over and people had begun to drift away, I joined the group still around Arcaro and found myself standing next to Church, whom I'd seen galloping or working horses every morning for the past few weeks in preparation for the race. I asked him what he thought his chances were. "I don't know," he said. "I won last year by getting out in front and the horse luckily kept going. You know, what you lose is your timing, your sense of pace. I had no idea how fast my horse was going or how big a lead I had. I never realized I had six lengths on the field and I kept looking back to see who was closing on me. The timing, it's the last thing to come back, even though you've been working horses in the morning. Maybe it never comes back."

The Rocking Chair Derby was run between the fifth and sixth races on the program the following Wednesday and a large, friendly crowd hemmed the paddock in to get a look at the riders. When they finally entered the ring, attired in their silks and looking, at first glance, pretty much like any other group of jockeys getting ready to race, they were greeted by a smattering of applause. Friendly voices called out to them. To Taniguchi, who now works as a placing judge at the track: "Hey, George, your vacation's over!" To Harmatz, who looked overweight and out of shape: "Hang on, Billy, hang on tight!" To Hall, who was sporting a full beard: "Shave it off, Dean, you're packing extra weight!" Hubert Trent, slim and straight and very serious about his task, with cheeks as red as the silks he wore, stood quietly by while Hector Palma spent several minutes explaining in detail how he wanted his problem horse handled. They were running here, after all, for a total purse of sixty-five hundred dollars, no mean sum, and Palma still hadn't allowed himself to be swept away by the romance of the event.

When the horses and riders appeared in front of the stands on their way to the post, track announcer Harry Henson introduced each rider and listed his achievements, though he was forced to quickly correct himself when he said about Harmatz that he was "an eighteen-year-old veteran" of the turf. Eddie Arcaro was introduced to the crowd, acknowledged the applause with a smile and a wave and quipped, "I'm not worried about picking a winner in this race. I'm worried about their staying on."

I got into a small betting pool with four friends of mine in the grandstand area and for two dollars picked Hubert Trent to win it all, not out of sheer sentiment either, but also because I thought he had a good chance. I knew Wally Laub could run a bit, if he felt like it, and Trent was the only rider out there who still earned his living on horseback. Sentiment can go a long way with me at the track, but I usually like to temper it with a little solid figuring.

The race itself was a beauty. The start out of the gate was clean and greeted by a roar of excitement from the crowd. Hall broke on top with his mount, but soon fell back and by the quarter pole Taniguchi, Church, and Neves had opened up a couple of lengths on the field in a battle for the lead. Wally Laub and Trent were pinned on the rail, but the horse was running willingly and I was sure he'd have a good shot at it, if he could find a hole to come through. At the half-mile, Trent got clear and moved into contention as they swung around the turn, half a length behind Taniguchi on Martizia. At the head of the stretch Wally Laub had taken the lead and looked like a sure winner, but he suddenly began to fade. Martizia came on again, stuck his head in front, then barely held on as Angel Valenzuela, on a horse called Dr. Robinson, came charging up between Wally Laub and Martizia and just missed winning by a head. Wally Laub finished third, beaten by a half-length, with The Bureaucrat and Ken Church another half-length back in fourth. It was by far the most exciting race of the day and the crowd roared its approval.

I went down by the finish line as the riders guided their mounts back. The old boys looked very tired and Neves, who had to be helped out of the saddle, looked ill. He'd had a headache before the race, I was told, and had been informed by Dan Smith that he could, of course, take off, but he'd insisted. "We got beat by a Chinaman," he grumbled, as he walked shakily over to the winner's circle to congratulate Taniguchi and pose for pictures with the other old-timers. "Beat by a goddam Chinaman."

"I got shut off," Angel Valenzuela kept saying to everyone within earshot. "I got shut off or I win it."

"Yeah, and you didn't get a chance to claim foul or nothin'," Arcaro said, grinning.

"Well, you guys, you're the stewards," Church said. "But then the whole world knows stewards can't see anything." He shook his head. "Anyway, my horse tore off half his hoof and come up empty."

"I got no complaints," Dean Hall observed happily. "I was never in trouble. I stayed outside all the way and I had a real good time."

"Hey, Angel," Arcaro called out, as the jockeys now began to group together in the winner's circle, "hey, what was that all about? You go between two horses for money, not for fun!"

The man having the most fun was George Taniguchi, who now lowered himself slowly and with evident relish into the large, brown rocker that had been set up in the winner's circle and faced the crowd. "It felt like I was in a hundred-thousand-dollar race," he said. "Boy, I was really all out at the end. I thought they were gonna catch me."

After the pictures were over and the crowd had begun to disperse, Hubert Trent walked up to Hector Palma, who had stayed behind to watch the ceremony and looked more relaxed, now that the race had been run. "I'm sorry, Mr. Palma," Trent said. "I'da won it, if I don't drop my stick at the quarter pole."

"It's all right," Palma said. "You did good."

The management threw a dinner dance that night on the clubhouse terrace, with a small band playing foxtrots and the guests seated outside under the stars. The evening was full of sentiment and laughs, as each rider was introduced by Arcaro, who kept the flow of jokes and small talk going. Dave Gorman, who had finished last on a horse appropriately named Old Memories, had drunk too much and kept shouting, "When are *you* coming back, Eddie? Why don't *you* come back, Eddie?" But nobody minded, really. Maybe Gorman hadn't heard about Arcaro's open-heart surgery. Maybe he'd forgotten. In any case, I suddenly remembered how Arcaro had looked the year before his retirement, lying motionless on the track at Belmont Park, the victim of a bad spill that had nearly cost him his life. No, he would never come back now and everyone in the place knew it except Dave Gorman, who was too drunk to remember or had never known much about Arcaro before this time at the Rocking Chair. "I rode when I had to," Arcaro had said earlier that day to a question by a reporter, "and when I got off, that was it." How could you blame him? Ralph Neves didn't make the party. He was home in bed that night, feeling rotten and so sore he could hardly move.

Later, on the way to my car, I passed Hubert Trent walking alone across the parking lot. He was neatly dressed in a business suit, his hair slicked back, his third-place trophy tucked under his arm. I congratulated him, but he didn't smile. "I'da won it," he said, "if I don't drop my stick."

"Well, there's always next year."

"Yes," he said sadly and we shook hands. I watched him disappear into the darkness. The next morning he'd be out there again, galloping somebody's horse around the track, lost among the hundreds of other riders still making a living out of horses and doing it the hard way.

15

I'd Cut All Them Sonsabitches

What Roy Colosia doesn't know about horses could be written on the head of a very small pin and wouldn't be worth knowing anyway. Furthermore, Roy would be the first to agree with this assessment of his expertise and can attest to it, at the drop of an innuendo, in a conversational outpouring of fifty or sixty thousand superbly chosen words. We were introduced one morning in the track kitchen and about two hours and four thousand anecdotes later I managed, ears ringing, to get out of there, but only on the promise that I'd be back in the near future to hear the three or four million other things Roy still had right on the tip of his tongue. He doesn't bother much with subtleties either and no time is wasted on false modesty. All Roy has to hear is your name and he's out of the gate and running.

"Yeah," he said, as we shook hands and I descended into a chair, "I'm what they call a livin' legend. I broke four

Kentucky Derby winners, only man who's ever done that. I was the first boy up on Whirlaway, who was just as nervous and fidgety as could be, which is because his Daddy Blenheim was like that and all his horses was the same, just as crazy as they could be. Well, this colt had broke the legs on four or five boys, the way he pitched, ya know, and Bill Molter, who had him then, he comes up to me and he says I was the only one could break him. Well, I climbed up on him and he'd flip me off, dumped me so many times I got these calluses on my butt and it took me four months to break that sonofabitch, but I broke him. Now, Shut Out, I not only broke him but I took him to the post on Derby day and he wasn't even the best horse in the race, which was his stablemate Devil Diver, but John Gaver screwed that up when he put the throat latch on too tight so you couldn't even get your hand underneath it, ya know, and Leigh Cotton, he come over and told Mr. Gaver he had it too tight, but he got told to mind his own business, so when the race got off Arcaro took a hold and just about choked the horse to death so he couldn't hardly breathe none. Now, I told the boy up on Shut Out when we was on the way to the post that you had to sting this horse left-handed and really get into the sonofabitch or he wouldn't run a lick, but you hit that sucker on his virgin side, why hell, he'll explode on ya, which is how come Shut Out win the Derby that year though that Devil Diver, God, he was a runnin' fool and maybe the better horse even that day, ya know? Now, you take Pensive. . . ." All this before I'd had my first sip of coffee. When Roy is out there winging, it's hard to keep up with him or do anything else but listen with the utmost attention, otherwise you get completely lost back there in that verbal dust storm he churns up and never do figure out who anybody is or what it all means.

The really miraculous thing about Roy Colosia is that none of the verbiage seems to interfere much with his other major pleasure in life, which is the nonstop consumption of huge, vile-looking cigars that he puffs on and keeps firmly clamped between his teeth as he orates. The morning we met he simply leaned back in his chair, a gray cap tilted to one side over a thick crop of spiky-looking hair, and let fly, the cigar jabbing the air in time to the tumultuous outpouring of his reminiscences and observations. We sat there long after everyone else around us had gone back to work and I found myself wondering, after a while, what could be keeping this supremely vigorous, energetic man in his early fifties from some far more urgent task than the enlightenment of an obvious dude like myself. I didn't get my answer until I finally staggered to my feet, protesting feebly that I really had to get back to my room and type up some notes. Roy nodded and, without dropping a syllable, rose to see me out. He's a cripple.

"Got this one leg that's now three inches shorter than the other one," he explained, limping heavily but easily keeping up with me as we walked to my car. "Happened on December 17, 1969. This gravel truck hit me and ran over me in San Dimas. They pronounced me dead four times, but I wasn't about to check out yet, though I was broke up pretty bad and the doctors told me I wouldn't never walk again, but hell, I wasn't buyin' that kind of talk neither. I'm gettin' around pretty good now—" and then, for the first time that morning, he paused, ever so slightly, but it was there—"still, about ridin' again," he continued, "I don't know. I just don't know about that."

He was born in 1921 in San Antonio, Texas, I found out later, and ran away from home when he was fourteen to gallop horses for a small racing outfit in Illinois. He came home the next year, but got picked up by truant officers for cutting school. It turned out, though, that the officers were not averse to cashing tickets and, instead of taking Roy to school every day, they'd whisk him out to the local track, Alamos Downs, where Roy knew practically everybody and could usually come up with a winner or two. The experience was the closest he ever came to having to resume a formal education, but it earned him a diploma with the truancy boys and got him into racing in a serious way. He decided to become a jockey.

It was the wrong decision, because he couldn't win a race. He just didn't have that "clock in his head," that innate talent that makes a race rider. His real ability, he soon discovered, was even rarer. He could break and ride any horse that ever lived, no matter how nervous, crazy, or mean the animal might be. In the winter of 1938, a cold and hungry one for a lot of Americans, he put together a team of five or six "good boys," including himself, and began to "contract-break" yearlings all over Kentucky. "We had this big old Buick," he recalled, "and we'd go up and down the state to all the farms, wherever, and we'd pull into a place and I'd ask how many they had. Well, maybe the fella would say, 'Roy, we got twenty head, eight colts and twelve fillies, and what'll you charge me to break 'em?' I'd try to figure real quick how many of 'em was gonna get sick on me or have to be wormed, 'cause I still wanted to get paid, and I'd come up with some sum like two or three thousand, depending, and then we'd get to it. We'd stay there six, seven, eight weeks, however long it took, and then we'd move on."

He also became known as a man who could handle even the worst rogues and outlaws, such as Trierarch, a gelding so mean that he once chewed two fingers off a groom out in front of the stands at Bay Meadows, in San Francisco, after a race back in the mid-forties, or Rawsun, a horse with a vile temper and a talent for demolishing the starting gate, as well as anyone incautious enough to get within reach of his teeth. "Yeah," Roy said, "I seen some real mean ones, but I never seen a horse that was born bad. The bad actors, they was made that way by some fella who didn't know how to handle 'em. The first thing with a horse or any animal is you don't show fear. An animal knows before you even get close to him if you're scared or not. A horse, he'll let ya know with his ears what's goin' on. You watch them ears and you'll be all right. If he pins 'em back, you know he's up to somethin' and you better anticipate it."

"So what else can you tell about a horse just by looking at him?" I asked.

"Everything," Roy said, "just about everything there is to know, if you know what you're lookin' at."

About halfway through the meet, in mid-August, the stock to be auctioned off at the annual California summer yearling sale began to arrive in Del Mar. The horses, about a hundred and fifty of them, were stabled in small, portable pens erected for the occasion on a parking lot across from the clubhouse and under a filtered, green awning that protected them from the weather. Behind it, the sales pavillion, a big tent striped in blue and yellow, arose over a sea of folding chairs facing a small, roped-off dirt ring flanked by the autioneer's stand. Here, on the night of August 19, most of the horses on hand would be sold to the highest bidders among the trainers, owners, and owners' agents present to try and pick up likely prospects for their racing stables. During the four days before the auction itself, prospective buyers could inspect the animals being offered simply by dropping in and taking a close look at them in their stalls.

I went by there myself to see what was going on the morning before the day of the sale and the first person I bumped into was Roy Colosia, teeth clamped on the inevitable cigar, temporarily out, and lips still going a mile a second. "I'm waitin' on this fella, he's supposed to be here by now, but I know him, he's always late," he said, "so come on now, let me show you around. They got a couple of nice-lookin' animals in here, though nothin' real special, but you can kind of get the feel of what to look for, ya know? You hear that sonofabitch tryin' to kick his stall down already? One starts up, they all do it. They been in here four days now and they're not used to bein' confined. Shit, I'd cut all them sonsabitches. Come on now, let's walk around."

It was very pleasant in there, strolling up and down between the long, straight rows of pens while Roy pumped a steady stream of information at me. The yearlings, still not full grown, paced restlessly in their stalls, their coats gleaming, or stood out in the aisles while their owners and keepers fussed over them. Every effort was being made to improve their looks, so that on the night of the sale itself they'd appear irresistible to the hard-eyed, cynical experts who'd appraise them and presumably bid on them when they were finally led into the bright sunshine of the spotlights focused on the auction ring. Each animal here was identified only by a so-called hip number, hung beside each stall along with a detailed breakdown of the horse's lineage on both sides and the accomplishments of those illustrious parents and ancestors. To most horsemen breeding is eighty percent of the game, which is why sires like Secretariat can be syndicated for millions of dollars and can command hundred-thousand-dollar stud fees even from the owners of top brood mares, whose weanlings will sell for as high as a quarter of a million dollars. Still, there is no guarantee of success, and buying a racehorse, no matter what its breeding, is essentially a crap shoot. Tracks all over the country are full of once high-priced horses now running in cheap claiming races, not to mention all the animals who never even get to the races at all. We had paid thirty thousand dollars for War Flag, I reminded myself, and lost him for a fifth of that amount. Horse-owning has always been a rich man's game.

We paused at the end of one aisle and watched a pretty girl gently walk a big, awkward-looking colt around in a tight circle. "See how that horse walks?" Roy growled. "Like a goddam cow! See that big belly on him? That means he's full of worms. See that big shoulder muscle right there? You got to cut his goddam nuts off to stop that growth. A horse this big, you got to wait till they're three and they fill out before you run 'em. Aw, shit, I wouldn't take him on a bet."

The girl noticed us talking and smiled at us. "He's beautiful, isn't he?" she said.

"Yes, ma'am," Roy said, "nice-lookin' colt ya got there."

"He's so sweet," the girl said. "I hope nobody takes him, 'cause I want him."

"These big colts are docile," Roy explained, as we resumed our walk. "They seem to love affection and need it. The little ones get pesty. They bite, they kick. They're like a little person, ya know? Strut around, shove their chests out at ya, just darin' ya to start somethin'."

We stopped in front of Hip No. 63, a chestnut colt born February 25, 1974. A stocky, placid-looking man who was acting as agent for the owners let us into the stall with him and stood by while Roy ran his hands over the animal's skin and checked the width of his head, the feel of his stomach. "Not a bad-lookin' colt," he said. "You oughta get ten thousand for this one."

"Hell," the agent said, "I sold this colt's brother for seventeen."

"Well, good luck to ya," Roy said, slapping the horse's rump and stepping out into the aisle again.

Hip No. 141 impressed Roy more than any of the others we'd seen that morning. "He's small," he said, "only about thirteen hands, but this is the kind of colt you wanna buy, what you call a perfectly balanced colt. See how wide he is behind? See how he walks? He's pesky, too. These small ones are durable. Feel his skin? He's been wormed, you can tell by the oil on your hands. A horse with worms, his skin'll be all dried up. Them worms can suck the life out of a horse. And you can't even see his nuts. This colt'll bring a pretty good piece of money."

We headed back at last toward the entrance, where Roy expected by now to find the potential buyer who wanted him to appraise some horses for him. I asked Roy before we parted why he seemed so obsessed by the presence of testicles on all the male horses we'd seen. " 'Cause most of 'em can't run with them nuts back there," he explained. "They get their minds on somethin' else, ya know, go studdish on ya. You remember that King of Cricket?"

"Sure," I said. "He's still running, isn't he?"

"Still holds the track record here for six furlongs," Roy said. "One-o-seven and three. I cut him. Jesus, he had a pair of nuts on him like cantaloupes. I'd cut all them sonsabitches, I tell ya."

The sale, held on the following afternoon and evening in two sessions, proved to be a success. A hundred and twenty-one of the yearlings offered were sold for a total of $1,265,400, or an average of $10,461 per horse. Hip No. 63 brought $15,400, while Hip No. 141, the animal Roy had liked best, went for only five thousand, a real bargain. I hung around for about half an hour at the evening session, but missed the only ugly incident of the day, when a fifty-five-year-old bidder suddenly collapsed with a heart attack and died there in his wife's arms.

Much later, I ran into Roy in the lobby of the Lodge. He was slumped into an armchair, the inevitable cigar in his mouth, but looking uncharacteristically distraught. His man had never showed up and Roy had missed out on a possible easy dollar, which was important to him because he now depended on such fringe benefits to get along. I offered to buy him a drink, but he shook his head and I decided he probably wanted to be left alone for a while. I had never seen him down before, but he was the sort of man, I guessed, who didn't need company or sympathy in adversity. I started to leave.

"Was you there when that fella keeled over?" he asked.

"No, but I heard about it. Who was he?"

"Some fella," Roy said. "His wife kept tellin' him 'Please don't die, please don't die!' Boy, she's gonna be pretty pissed off by the time she catches up to him."

16

Leave Them Laughing, Even If It Hurts

A couple of days after the yearling sale, a nice old black man named Alvin McCullough tried to sell me a horse. He caught me at a very bad time, even if I had had the money, which I didn't. I had just lost my fifth consecutive photo finish and I was walking away from the track in disgust to cut my losses for the day when McCullough caught up to me, near the clubhouse gate. "Say, Bill," he said, smiling sweetly, "how you doin'?"

"Terrible," I told him. "Let's not talk about it."

McCullough had no intention of talking about it; he had bigger things on his mind than my betting woes. He'd been training a few horses for a man who'd just run out on his stable bills and was holed up in a hotel room somewhere in San Diego, apparently permanently drunk. "He'll have to show up sometime," was McCullough's reasoning, "but he ain't got no money and somebody could prob'ly pick up this little two-year-old filly of his real cheap right now."

I trusted McCullough. He was one of the very few black trainers in California and, like the others, not doing too well. (The racing establishment out here is strictly WASP.) I had met him through a friend of mine named Joe Ward, a black medical technician who also dabbles in equine matters, and Joe had convinced me that the old man knew what he was about. Joe had hung around McCullough's barn in his spare time during the late spring and had helped him improve the performances of a couple of cheap runners McCullough trained, but this disappearing owner of his had suddenly left Alvin high and very dry. He wanted somebody to buy the filly for him so he could go on training her. "I worked her a quarter in twenty-three and three and then three-eighths in thirty-six flat at Pomona," he said. "Now you know that's good time there, with those sharp turns. But then she bucked a shin and I had to back off her. Now I got her ready to go again, but I can't even take her out of her stall to gallop her."

I told McCullough that I was in no position to buy any part of a horse again at the moment, but I'd ask around for him. "What's her breeding?"

"Her breeding's not much," he admitted. "She's by Azcay out of a Rideabout mare. But, you know, I don't put too much stock in breeding. I tell ya this little filly can run. That's what matters, isn't it?"

Yes, that's what matters, all right. The sudden unexpected chance, however improbable, to get back in action with a horse of my own jabbed sharply at my memory. It

was a cheap little horse, after all, that had given me my
very best times at the track.

By the end of the War Flag saga, in the late spring of
1968, three of the original five partners in our stable admitted to being a little winded. Duke, Al, and Howard
decided, in fact, that they had had enough and went back
to civilian life, taking what was left of their investment
with them. Jerry and I surveyed the debris that passed
for our bank account and discovered that we now had
about four thousand dollars left. We decided we might as
well shoot craps and began to look around for a cheap
horse to claim from somebdy else.

The one we selected had an interesting name, El Lobo,
but, judging by his record, little else to recommend him;
he hadn't even come close to winning a race in over a
year. But Reavis picked one small statistic out of the
Racing Form and indicated it to us, jabbing at it with a
stubby forefinger in the track cafeteria at Hollywood Park
the morning El Lobo was scheduled to run in a four-thou-
sand-dollar claiming race. "Look here," the trainer said,
"this sucker worked a mile in one thirty-nine flat. Hell, he
works faster than these other horses in here with him can
run."

He didn't run much that day, finishing fourth against
the worst horses on the grounds, but just before the race
we dropped our last four thousand dollars into the claim
box and took him. "Well, that wipes us out," I said cheer-
fully to Jerry, feeling an odd sense of relief, as if I'd suddenly become impregnable to further disaster. If I'd

known what the next few months held in store, I'd have
invested immediately in an oxygen mask.

About ten days later, on July 10, El Lobo ran his first
race for us. The distance was a mile and one-sixteenth and
he was in against slightly better horses than he'd just lost
to. I gave him no chance but bet fifty dollars on him anyway, out of foolhardy sentiment. I didn't pay much attention to the early part of the race, but as the field hit the
turn for home I suddenly realized that our jockey Bill
Harmatz had El Lobo rolling along the outside and they
were picking up one horse after another. I began to
scream. By the time El Lobo hit the finish line, a couple
of lengths in front, I had laryngitis. But who cared? We
had just won three thousand dollars in purse money and
my fifty-dollar bet had been on the nose at a delicious
sixteen to one. "What did you do, Willis?" I asked, as we
rushed for the winner's circle.

"Just changed his shoes is all," said Reavis, that genius.
"The dumb bastard that had him had the wrong shoes on
him. Why he couldn't hardly walk in 'em."

Eight days after that, El Lobo came out again in his new
shoes. He was up another notch in company and at the
shorter distance of seven furlongs, which didn't figure to
favor his late-running style. I didn't care. I had returned
to the true faith and I'd have bet El Lobo that day against
a Ferrari. I put two hundred dollars on him at nine to one.

Once again El Lobo started late and finished like an
express train, zooming past the front-runner, a game and
still talented ex-stakes horse, to win by a long neck in excellent time. Jerry and I threw our arms around each other
and danced the wild fandango to the cashiers' windows.

Oh, may this never end, I said to myself, may this never, never, never end!

It did, of course, but very honorably. Reavis gave El Lobo a short, well-merited rest, then took him down to Del Mar for the summer meeting. He entered the horse in an eight-thousand-dollar claiming event at a mile. The field was short, with only six horses in it, and two of them were ailing but classy beasts being dropped down in company in an effort to win a purse. "I wouldn't bet him in there," Jerry said. "He doesn't figure to beat those two top horses, the odds with this short field will be low and we stand to pick up a piece of the purse anyway. He should run third."

Jerry proved to be a seer. El Lobo finished a very respectable third, but it was the last race he ran for us. Farrell Jones, a trainer with a huge public stable, claimed him from us, as somebody figured to. Trainers like Jones are always looking for improving animals, horses "on their way up the ladder," to claim for their many owners. But could I complain? Hardly. In six weeks, between purses won, doubling our money on the original claim price and bets cashed, I had recouped all of my losses with War Flag. Still, I wanted Reavis to watch for a chance to get El Lobo back from Jones. "I wouldn't," the trainer said. "He ain't that sound and Jones'll run him into the ground."

El Lobo never won a race for Jones or for anybody else, as far as I know. The last time I saw him on the track, some months later, the hairs on his front legs were tightly curled, indicating that he'd probably been standing for hours in ice, and he walked as if tiptoeing on glass. Trainers like Jones and Frankel, who win more races year after year than anybody else, do so, usually, at the expense of their animals. They pump them full of butazolidin and other pain-killers, inject them with cortisone, baste them in iodine, anything to get winning races out of them. By the time they're through with an animal there's nothing left but dog meat. But then horse racing is a business, you soon discover, not a sport.

The highest gambling wisdom is knowing when to quit. El Lobo, however, had scrambled my brains. I was like a man panning for gold in a riverbed who's just found the world's biggest nugget and some ass comes along, waving his arms and shouting that the dam upstream is about to burst. Do you get out of the water and head for the high ground? Of course not. So over the next eighteen months of my career as a horseowner came the deluge. Oh, we clawed up on dry land a couple of times, but never long enough to get toasty. The fates, as usual, were diddling with us.

There was, for instance, the case of Quita Dude. He was a nine-year-old gelding we took out of a cheap claiming race at Del Mar because Reavis was sure he could win with him. He had had the horse years before, when he was good and had won a couple of important races. "I know how this big sucker likes to run," the trainer said. "He should beat this kind walkin'."

Quita Dude was a monster. Not only was he the biggest horse I'd ever seen, he was easily the fussiest. Here are Reavis' instructions to Alex Maese, the jockey who rode him for us the first time: "You got to take a big hold on him out of the gate and pull him back away from all the other horses or he's going to fight you and try to run with 'em. He's got one move in him and it's exactly three-eighths of a mile. You got that? Good. Now take him back and let him relax. It don't matter how far he drops out of it or what the pace is, just don't let him run early. Then, when you hit the three-eighths pole, let him go. He'll come like a hurricane."

Maese stared at Reavis as if the trainer had just tried to peddle him a platinum soup plate. "There's one other thing I didn't tell him," Reavis added, as we watched Maese guide Quita Dude toward the starting gate. "This horse won't run on the inside neither. He don't like the dirt kicked up into his face and he hangs."

"Why didn't you tell Maese that?" I asked.

" 'Cause what I told him is bad enough," the trainer said. "Hell, you can't ask no rider to take back thirty lengths and then tell him to go wide on the turn. He'll think you're crazy."

Evidently Maese didn't believe a word of what Reavis had told him, because he ran Quita Dude up with the leaders for the first half-mile and wound up last. We tried a couple of more times with other riders, but the conditions were never met. Either the jockey wouldn't take Quita Dude far enough back or he'd move him too soon or he'd try to come through on the inside. By the time Del Mar ended and the horses moved to Pomona for the traditional two weeks of racing on the grounds of the L.A. County Fair, I'd given up hope, especially because I was certain Quita Dude would never get up in time around the tight turns of that half-mile track, which favors front-running speed horses.

Miguel Yanez, the Mexican jockey who rode Quita Dude

at Pomona, listened to Reavis' spiel with the stony impassivity of an Aztec carving. He mounted and rode off without a word or even a nod and Reavis observed that he probably didn't understand English. I bet only twenty dollars on Quita Dude, so, of course, he won, at astronomical odds and exactly the way he was supposed to, coming from a mile out of it and looping the field on the turn. "Sure he understands English," I said, clapping Reavis on the back.

"No, he don't," said the trainer. "The horse had his head turned when the gate opened, so he got left. And with these tight turns there ain't no way you can come through on the inside. There wasn't nothin' Yanez could do to fuck it up."

"Maybe we should let the horses run on their own," Jerry said. "These damn jocks are a handicap."

Two weeks later, Quita Dude hurt himself in training and we eventually sold him for a fraction of what we'd paid and put into him. But by this time we had nothing but losses to add up anyway. There was Climb Across, a three-year-old who won one race for us at Del Mar in very slow time and moved speedily on to oblivion. There was Camaro, a horse I distrusted from the first because he'd been named after a mediocre car and who never won a race for us before he, too, injured himself and had to be sold at a tidy deficit. And there was Parlay Time, a horse I claimed on my own without Jerry and who turned out to be the world's champion wind-sucker. He'd gnaw for hours on anything solid within reach and, while doing so, suck in great gulps of air, bloating himself so that he couldn't eat or train properly. I sold him to a lady who wanted a saddle horse and she had to put him in a metal stall charged to give him a shock every time he went to work playing with himself. I hope she cooked him.

Last, but certainly not least in the freak parade, was Irish Friendship, a six-year-old male with his sex organs intact. "That's good," I said. "If we still have him when he's through racing, we can use him as a stud. He's got some breeding."

"No, you can't," Reavis answered. "This horse don't like mares. He only likes ponies. He just loves them ponies. You get him near a pony and he'll mount him. On the track the outriders all know about him. He's kind of a joke."

"Christ," Jerry said, "we got us a fag horse."

The fag could run, though. However, he was really bad-legged and the problem was keeping him sound. He won the race we claimed him out of, then he picked up pieces of purses for us here and there while Reavis tried to find just the right spot for him to win one. Before he could do so, Irish Friendship stepped into a hole while training and bowed a front tendon. Next to a broken bone, a bowed tendon is the most serious injury that can overtake a race-horse. It requires a minimum of six months to heal and, even if he does get back to the races, the horse is rarely ever as good again and will often bow a second time after a few more races.

Irish Friendship received the best of medical care and was shipped off to an expensive ranch to convalesce. Jerry and I, by this time, were struggling to get out from under our other losses, but we decided to wait for Irish to come back. "We'll take him down to Tijuana and run him there," Jerry said. "He'll have been away a long time, his workouts never show much and he looks fat. This horse has so much class that on three legs he can beat what they got running down in Mexico. We should get a big price on him and get some of our money back betting on him."

It took fifteen months for Irish Friendship to come back. His training was taken over at Caliente by a plump, pink-cheeked Munchkin named Bobby Warren. "My God, look at the belly on him," he said when he first saw the horse. "This one must drink more beer than I do."

Warren took another ninety days to get some of the belly off our horse and put him into a sprint race, in which he had no chance, to tighten him. "He's got some problems," he confided to us, "but he can run, all right. Only you may lose him. There's a group comes up from Mexico City every weekend looking for studs."

"That's all right," Jerry said and told Warren about our horse's predilection for ponies. "Anyway, we don't care. Just hold him together for one more race, that's all we ask."

The great day finally came and Jerry and I brought six hundred dollars, the last of our stable's bank account, down to Tijuana. Irish Friendship was entered in a sixteen-hundred-dollar claiming race at a mile and a sixteenth against pigs he'd have eaten alive the year before. Best of all, it was a Quinella race, meaning that we could win a goodly amount of money by picking two horses in the field to finish one–two in any order. We coupled Irish Friendship, who went off at nine to one, with every other horse in the race in varying amounts; all he had to do was finish second and we were back in business with a fattened bank account.

"This horse don't look like much but he can run," Bobby

Warren told our jockey, Raul Caballero, who was considered one of Caliente's top riders. "He'll be a little short, so don't move till the half-mile pole. And don't worry about having to come on the outside because he'll outrun all these others. Just don't get boxed in and don't make him run too early."

The race went off and Irish Friendship dropped behind the leaders around the first turn. As they straightened out for the run down the backstretch, however, he suddenly began to move so fast it looked as if the other horses were running on a treadmill. "Look at him go!" I shouted.

"It's too early," Jerry said. "That asshole is moving him much too soon."

At the head of the stretch Irish Friendship was two lengths in front, but he was beginning to shorten stride and the field was closing on him. Still, all he had to do was finish second and we'd be big winners. Jerry and I screamed encouragement, but in vain. A few yards from home Irish got caught and passed. He finished third.

Warren, who had also bet heavily on him, was livid. "What the hell was that dumb bastard of a jock thinking about?" he said.

"I don't know," Jerry answered. "If a man had any brains, he wouldn't be risking his life on the backs of dumb animals anyway."

Irish Friendship did not come out of the race well and Warren informed us the next day that he didn't think the horse had more than two or three outings left in him. "Drop him down to the bottom and let's unload him," Jerry said. So, a week later, Irish Friendship was entered for a claiming tag of a thousand dollars at the same distance.

He won easily that day, but Jerry and I didn't bet on him. He was the heavy favorite and we were out of money. We stood by the rail near the finish line and silently watched him come home in front and I think the same thought was going through our heads. We had started out with a thirty-thousand-dollar horse with a win at a major track and dreams of the Kentucky Derby. Now here we were, two and a half years later, ending the adventure with another victory, but this time with a crippled plater at a third-rate track and no dreams at all. Also no money. The six-hundred-dollar purse we'd just won bailed us out of our stable bill with Warren and we went north empty-handed. I estimated later that overall I had dropped a total of about fifteen thousand dollars as a horse owner, which is the kind of tax deduction only writers like Philip Roth and Mario Puzo can afford.

Irish Friendship was claimed out of his winning race by the outfit from Mexico City. As a courtesy, Warren dropped by the new stable to inform them of their horse's peculiarities. The sour Texan who trained for the stable cut Warren off early. "We know how to handle horses," he said. "We don't need no advice." Warren shrugged and left.

The next time Irish Friendship came out to run, he was accompanied onto the track by an outrider on a honey-colored pony. And right there, in front of the packed stands, Irish Friendship threw off his rider and mounted the beautiful pony. He was scratched from the race. We heard about it that night from Warren and I wish I'd been there to see it. It handed me one of the biggest laughs I ever had out of horse racing.

17

All for Sport

The first really bad spill of the meeting took place on August 24, a Sunday, when a fast four-year-old filly named Star Balla went down shortly after she broke out of the gate. She was on the lead at the time and the horses behind her were lucky to be able to avoid her, but her jockey, Raul Ramirez, hit the ground very hard. He lay there while the rest of the field swept past him and he did not get up. I could just make out the tiny patch of his gold silks and white breeches lying there in the dirt before he was surrounded by several of the assistant starters, who had run up the track from the gate, and a couple of people who had clambered out of the guinea stand to get to him. An ambulance was already circling the outside of the clubhouse turn and the meat wagon was on its way from the stable area for Star Balla. The filly was struggling to get up, but she couldn't make it and was obviously in terrible distress. By the time the rest of the horses in the race reached the finish line, Ramirez was being carefully loaded onto a stretcher and two men were trying to do what they could to calm the injured horse.

Bellona, the seven-to-two second choice, won the race, but many in the crowd booed the result. Star Balla had been the less well-regarded half of an entry that had gone off at even money. Bill Shoemaker, the rider on Lilol-schoolteacher, Star Balla's stablemate, had had to check his horse in order to avoid the inert Ramirez and so had lost all chance of winning. The plungers who had bet on him didn't like that at all, so they booed. A few people didn't even stop booing when the ambulance carrying Ramirez, its red emergency lights flashing, turned past the stands and drove out through the gap beside the clubhouse.

Luckily no one was forced to watch what had to be done to Star Balla to get her into the wagon and carted away to be put out of her misery. Through my glasses I could see that one of her front legs flopped uselessly about, held on only by skin and tissue. Having to watch such a scene while people boo is to be witness to a public obscenity, but then whoever said that racing is a sport and that men are kind? On the day that the great filly Ruffian broke down in her match race with Foolish Pleasure last year, a jockey named Juan Gonzales was killed during a race in San Francisco. The sports pages and all the network news shows were full of Ruffian stories and two women I know and love actually cried when they heard what had happened to her. The news of Juan Gonzales' death qualified for one small paragraph in the *Los Angeles Times* and a short piece in the *Form*. He was one of the leading riders on the northern California circuit. I have not read or heard his name mentioned since.

Very early on the morning after Star Balla went down and Ramirez was taken to the hospital, I had an appointment in the backside racing office with Alan Edmondson, the veterinarian at the track appointed by the California Horse Racing Board. There are usually at least a dozen vets working at any track during a meet and I had already met a couple of Edmondson's colleagues, including an older man who had been around for nearly a half-century and was considered an "ornament and a credit to the great sport of racing," to quote from a piece I'd once read about him. I had told the ornament that I wanted to make some rounds with him one day and he'd agreed, but without much enthusiasm. I'd spoken to him about it a couple of times since and he never said no, but always stalled me. But I'd decided by that time that I didn't trust him anyway. He had the tiny shrewd eyes of a small-town ward heeler and the poker-faced cynicism of a man who's seen too much and made too many compromises, so I finally asked Dan Smith to introduce me to Edmondson, whom I'd heard good things about from every horseman I'd talked to. He readily agreed to let me tag along with him one morning, but warned me that he started promptly at seven and liked to move fast.

When I arrived at the racing office just before the hour, I found Edmondson impatiently awaiting me. He's middle-aged and pink-cheeked and his thinning black hair is slicked straight back. He wear gold-rimmed eyeglasses that look precariously perched and reminds me of an old bit player from almost any old Judy Garland–Mickey

Rooney movie, perhaps one of the more conservative profs at the school where Judy and Mickey are about to put on a smash Broadway musical instead of wasting time on their homework. But appearances can be deceptive. Edmondson, I soon decided, was actually a track star; he moves around with what passes for unconcern, but at close to the speed of light. He's a busy man, I soon gathered, with responsibilities and little time to waste.

After a quick handshake, Edmondson whisked me inside, where an official handed him three pink slips on which three different trainers had given reasons for wanting to take their horses out of that day's card. Only the track vet or the stewards themselves can permit such late scratches and then usually only for medical reasons. Evan Jackson, for instance, a very conservative trainer with good stock but a low winning percentage, didn't want to run a filly of his named Dangerous Bluff in the feature because, as he put it, "I would rather wait for an easier race." I couldn't blame him, as he had unexpectedly drawn in against Miss Tokyo and Miss Musket, two of the more highly rated horses on the grounds, but Edmondson proved unsympathetic. "Not good enough," he snapped, handing the slip back to the official. "He's stuck." Trainers Junior Nicholson and John Parisella, however, wanted to take their two-year-old maidens out of the fourth race for what sounded like more legitimate reasons, so Edmondson tucked the remaining two slips into his pocket and we set off for Nicholson's barn, the nearer of the two, at a rapid dogtrot.

The trainer wasn't there, but his ailing horse, Hemp Ruler, was on the mechanical hot-walker and Edmondson got a groom to unhitch him and bring him over to where we stood. As Nicholson had claimed, the vet soon established that there was, indeed, some filling in the left hind leg. As he knelt by the animal and examined him, Edmundson also found another trouble spot. At his touch the horse suddenly jerked his leg away, just as Nicholson himself, plump and worried-looking, came around the corner of the barn. "Hello, Junior," the vet said. "Yeah, we'll have to take him out. That curb is tender, too. You'll have to blister him."

"One damn thing after another," Nicholson said. "This horse has never been quite right."

"Isn't that the way," Edmondson said, scribbling on the pink slip and starting to move on. "Got another one to check in this race."

"Who's that?" Nicholson called out.

"Parisella's colt," the vet barked. "See you, Junior."

During our brisk trot to Parisella's barn, which happened to be directly across the stable area but nearer the frontside, Edmondson told me his family had come to California around 1880 and settled in Pasadena, where he grew up. "I first went to the track as a boy in the mid-thirties," he said, "and some old horseman told me there were two types of guys who made money at the track—blacksmiths and vets. That tip sort of stuck with me and I soon realized there were very few horse doctors around. There wasn't even a vet school in California, so I went to Texas A & M, got my degree there, came back, and I've been here ever since." He got married, had two girls, and stayed on in Pasadena until a few years ago, "when the smog drove me out." He now lives in Huntington Beach, where presumably the air is clearer, and commutes to the tracks—no chore, I felt sure, for a man who moves as fast as he does.

Bobby Frankel was leaning against the corner of his barn and looking characteristically surly, but he nodded to us as we zipped past.

"How's that horse today?" the vet asked.

"About the same," Frankel said. "He just stands there, with his head down."

"He's referring to Sally's Date, the horse scratched out of the ninth yesterday," Edmondson explained, as we moved on. "There's something wrong with that horse, but the trick is finding out what. There's about a thousand ways a horse can go wrong and no easy way to find out what's ailing him."

I asked Edmondson why so many sore horses were allowed to run every day, just to see if I could get a rise out of him, but it didn't work. He only muttered something about "wrong priorities" and clearly looked uncomfortable. I gathered that he didn't think very highly of most of his colleagues, but wasn't about to say so to a man writing a book. He got out of the dilemma by getting into a brief conversation with Johnny Adams, who came riding past us on his way back from a workout. The two men had known each other for a long time and were obviously charter members of a mutual admiration society. A few minutes later, after Adams had ridden off, we passed an open doorway where old Buster Millerick stood, grinding the stub of an ancient spent cigar between his teeth and glaring out at the world from under a battered old hat that I felt sure he also slept in. Millerick is a small, pear-shaped man with the complexion of a radish and the temperament of a wolverine and his last big horse was Native Diver, one of the great champions of the California turf. Buster has a reputation for not tolerating owners who persist in hanging around and asking a lot of dumb questions, but he's undeniably a good trainer, maybe one of the best, and reputedly kind to children, small animals, and cute blondes. He and Edmondson growled and mumbled at each other as we swept past, but old Buster obviously belonged to the same confraternity as Johnny Adams.

When we'd turned a corner and were out of earshot, Edmondson pursed his lips thoughtfully, then said, "Johnny and Buster, they're two of the best. They don't send out sore horses." I didn't answer, but waited for him to enlighten me. "About what you said a few minutes ago," he continued, after another pause. "Let's just say that there are a lot of guys who train horses, but only about twelve of them are real horsemen. The rest range from standard to poor."

"And the vets?"

"The vets get paid to keep horses sound enough to run," he said and dropped the subject.

In Parisella's barn, we found the trainer in a swivet. Parisella is a tall, gangly New Yorker with a wild mop of unruly black hair and a Bowery accent. He's also a master of the non sequitur and initiates conversations at whatever point in his train of thought happens to strike his fancy. "You know what you are in this business, I told this guy," he said the moment he saw us. "I said you're a chump! In your own business maybe you're a king, but in this one you're a chump, a real *putz!* And this bum takes it off of

me, too! See, I knew about him, I knew his previous record, but I thought, you know, Del Mar, what the hell! So
I give the bum a chance! Well, he can go and get himself
a new boy, you know?"

"What's the trouble, John?" Edmondson asked. "What
happened?"

"What happened? What *happened?*" Parisella said,
snorting and flailing his arms about. "I'll tell you what
happened! This bum, he comes in here about twelve-thirty
and he wants to know how come nobody's around. So the
girl that works for me, she's here, and she tells him it's
twelve-thirty, for Christ's sake, and who should be around?
So you know what this bum does? He takes one of his
horses that I got bandaged and I'm working on him and
he walks the horse around! I mean, how do you like this
guy? I told him to get his goddam horses out of here like
today, you know? This chump, that's what he is, a chump
with a capital P!"

The "chumP," I found out later, was an owner who had
recently turned his horses over to Parisella and had a reputation for being difficult. He was a retired contractor, I was
told, and had a wife who was more trouble than he was,
which seemed improbable, judging from the splendid performance the man had goaded out of his trainer.

Edmondson examined Nevada Don, the colt Parisella
wanted to take out of the fourth race, and found that his
shins had bucked. "OK, John, he comes out," the vet said.

"This bum!" Parisella continued. "Can you imagine the
nerve of this guy?"

"John's new out here," Edmondson said, as we headed

back. "He hasn't had a chance to work through the squirrels yet."

We stopped by the racing office long enough for Edmondson to officially take Hemp Ruler and Nevada Don out of their race, then we scooted back to the guinea stand, where the vet stopped long enough to chat with a handful of old cronies up there to watch their horses work. I stood by, trying to catch my breath. "Say, Ed, what about Star Balla?" somebody asked.

"Her leg just snapped clean off," the vet said. "She must have stepped into a hole or something."

"How's the boy? I heard he's all right."

"Yep. Two horses went right over him, but he's just bruised, is all. Shoe was able to take up and went around him."

"Maybe that's why they booed him," someone else said.

"They boo him for everything," Edmondson said. "They'll boo him on the day he gets himself killed."

Five days later, in the fifth race on August 30, a horse named El Seetu, trained by Charlie Whittingham, fell on the turn for home and spilled Shoemaker into the turf. He fell hard, but luckily the turf course at Del Mar is relatively soft and deep. The jockey lay there for a few minutes, to make sure he was all right, then got up and walked off under his own power. He could easily have chosen not to ride again that day, but he saw no reason not to. In fact, he rode in three of the last four races and won the ninth on another Whittingham horse, beating my old favorite Burgeon. I happened to be in the paddock with Reavis when the horses were brought in before the race and

Whittingham hoisted his great rider into the saddle. "Hey, Shoemaker," someone in the crowd shouted, "go break a leg in this one!" A lot of people laughed. A few people even applauded.

18

An Electrical Storm

They had a very funny race here early in the meeting. I'd heard a sensational story about it at the time but had discounted it, until I was reminded again of the odd circumstances later on when a journeyman jock named Raul Cespedes was suspended five racing days by the stewards for "violation of California Horse Racing Board Rule 1690." Cespedes, according to the story in the *Racing Form*, was seen "to be in possession of a plastic 'goad' following his ride aboard favored Face the Sun last Friday in the third race." Face the Sun went off at eight to five and did not win; he tired in the stretch and finished third behind two big longshots, but somebody had had enough confidence in the horse to bet heavy money on him.

I knew something about Face the Sun, having seen him run a number of times. He was a speed horse who liked to get out in front, but he usually quit. He had yet to win a race and had been listed at three to one in the Morning

Line, a much more reasonable estimate of his chances against an admittedly undistinguished field of cheap maidens going a mile and a sixteenth. For him to be such a heavy favorite, however, somebody had to be betting with a confidence not generated by anything visible to the naked eye in his past-performance record.

A goad is a small plastic object slightly over two inches long and three-eighths of an inch wide, with a blunt edge. It looks much like a droplet and the rider uses it by jabbing it into the neck of his mount, the basic idea being to keep a tiring horse going or wake a lazy one up. They caught Cespedes with his when the race was over, after he'd dismounted and was unsaddling his horse. No official at the track the day the suspension was announced could immediately recall the last occasion a rider here had been caught using an illegal device in a race, though everybody in the press box remembered the time, a few years ago, when a much better-known jockey riding at Del Mar drew a life suspension for using a battery.

When Barry Irwin went around to ask the stewards about their ruling on Cespedes, they were at first reluctant to talk to him. Such incidents are not conducive to shoring up public confidence in the sport, after all, but Barry did finally get statements out of two of the three officials, Peder Pederson and Morton Lipton. "We want to put all riders on notice that we don't want them to use anything illegal on a horse," Pederson declared. "This particular device, in our opinion, did not affect the outcome of the race in question in any way. We insist that there was no unfair advantage taken of the public. Our main concern was to alert other riders that this type of situation will not be tolerated."

Lipton, who used to be a trainer, was asked to comment on the effectiveness of the goad. "It is exceedingly minor in comparison to an electrical device, which has a strong, powerful application," he said. "There is considerable doubt if the object in question has any effect whatsoever."

After reading this story, apart from being charmed by the convoluted officialese in which these gentlemen express themselves in public, I found myself wondering why a rider like Cespedes, who's been around a while, would risk his career to use such an apparently ineffective, not to say totally useless object. That quite naturally got me to thinking about this funny race I'd seen some weeks earlier and the delightful story I'd heard about it.

The event was an unimportant one for cheap claiming horses at a mile and a sixteenth, the field was small, and two of the horses were heavily favored; they were expected to run one–two, though in what order nobody could be quite sure. The horse I'll call Hurricane Joe was an ailing old gelding who had once had some class and had been showing signs recently of coming around. He invariably ran on the lead and the question was very simply whether he would stay there or not. Once hooked and passed, Hurricane Joe almost always lost interest and faded. His chief rival, whom I'll call Lochinvar, had once been a stakes horse, but he'd been away for over a year after various injuries and he showed slow works in the *Form*. Both animals were ridden by veteran Latin riders,

whom I'll call Don José and Escamillo. I had looked at
the race the night before in the *Form* and had decided not
to bet it.

I changed my mind the next morning, when I came
upon an old racetrack pal of mine named Artie. He was
lying around the pool at the Lodge, flanked by two plati-
num-headed Hollywood party girls in microscopic bikinis,
and he seemed to be enjoying himself hugely. We chatted
about this and that, while the platinum-heads oiled acres
of firm, pink skin, and my mind was starting to wander
into purely carnal areas when I heard Artie say, "You're
gonna bet my horse, ain't ya?" It turned out that he was one
of the owners of Lochinvar. His trainer, a knowledgeable
sort I'll call Winkie, had assured him the animal would
probably win and certainly run no worse than second. The
beast was unsound and had no more than two or three
races in him, but this was going to be the day to cash in.

Ordinarily I don't pay much attention to tips, but I made
an exception for Artie. I had known him for eight years,
having once accidentally shared a box with him at Santa
Anita for a few days, and he had never yet given me bad
information. The previous year, in fact, I had wheeled another of his crippled horses in a Daily Double on his
say-so and had walked out of the track five hundred dollars
richer. I also knew better than to pester him with questions. What I really wanted to do was sit down and help
his companions with their oil jobs, but I thanked him
instead and told him I'd see him at the track. "In my
business," Artie had once said to me, "murder is a mis-
demeanor." I've never asked him what his business was

and I don't want to know, nor do I ever want to make the mistake of moving in on his R and R personnel.

I bet a hundred dollars, divided equally between win and place, on Lochinvar and watched the race from the press box. As expected, Don José hustled Hurricane Joe to the lead and held it most of the way around the track, with Escamillo and Lochinvar somewhere back in the pack. On the far turn, Artie's horse began to move. At the head of the stretch, he caught and passed Hurricane Joe and opened up nearly a length with only about a sixteenth of a mile to go. I was counting my winnings when, to my amazement, Hurricane Joe suddenly came on again along the rail, swept past Lochinvar and won by two lengths, going away. I had never seen this horse do that before and surmised that Lochinvar must have broken down again and stopped, though the time of the last fraction didn't seem to indicate this possibility. I consoled myself by cashing my place bet, which netted me a few dollars, and felt sorry for Artie, who had probably lost his horse again.

"Are you kiddin'?" Artie roared at me, when I saw him the next day, minus the platinum heads. "Sure the horse broke down, but *after* the race. Let me tell you a story."

Artie had been standing at the rail by the winner's circle when the horses came back and he saw Winkie, who had gone out on the track, step on something, look at it, pick it up, and hastily stuff it into his pocket. Artie caught up to his trainer on their way back upstairs and nudged him. "I didn't know we was usin' equipment," he said. "I see you found it."

Winkie shook his head. "It ain't ours," he said. "It must be Don José's."

Later than night, at the bar of the Lodge, Artie spotted Don José sitting alone in a booth; he went over and sat down with him. "Hey, kid," Artie said, "Winkie found your equipment today."

Don José's eyes opened wide. "Oh, yes?" he said. "Oh, man, that ees the best wan I evair had. I got to get eet back. You got to get eet for me, all right?"

"I'll see what I can do," Artie said. "You oughta be more careful. Next time you better throw it away on the turn."

"Yes," the jockey agreed, "that was dumb, no?"

"Yeah," Artie said. "If I get it back for ya, you don't use it again on me, you understand?"

"*Si,*" Don José said, grinning. "No."

"So I got it back for him," Artie told me.

"Winkie gave it back?"

"Sure, why not?" Artie said. "Our boy had one, too. We got the Eveready concession down here, pal. Say, you got four, five riders use them all the time at this track. Shit, man, they shoot so much juice comin' down the stretch someday they're gonna shortcircuit the fuckin' tote board."

I'd had only one prior experience with jockeys using electrical devices, which are simply batteries with hot wires attached to them, and that was in Elko, Nevada, a few years ago. I'd gone up there to do a story for *Holiday* on northeastern Nevada and I found myself in this wild cattle town in the middle of nowhere over Labor Day weekend, when the place was packed with people in from all over for the annual County Fair, a leading feature of which was four days of horse racing. "What kind of horses do they have?" I asked the grizzled clerk at my hotel.

"All kinds," he said. "It ain't like your type of racin',
Mister. They ride right down to the nuts here."

I went out the next day and sat in a box the hotel had
bought for its guests and couldn't cash a ticket. The races
were run on a half-mile track that spewed up great clouds
of dust into which the horses—Thoroughbreds, cow ponies,
Appaloosas, goats, anything with four feet—disappeared
and did inexplicable things before lurching home in gla-
cially slow time. The odds on each entry were chalked up
on a big blackboard and were changed by hand depending
on the drift of the betting, as relayed by teams of scrawny,
jean-clad teenagers shuttling back and forth from the
board to the betting windows. A fifty-dollar wager on an
eight to one shot could shave the price to even money, I
soon realized, and there was no way to get a past line on
the horses, most of which were ancient and belonged to
itinerant hustlers skilled in the cunning ways of the smaller
fair circuits.

I was advised by my grizzled clerk to get into the stable
area and talk to a couple of people, whose names he gave
me. I got up very early the next morning and spent several hours among the horsemen, just listening. By post time
I had every race narrowed down to no more than two
horses and I swept the card. I repeated this procedure
the third and fourth days, with continued success, and
even found myself betting money for some of the boys
back there who didn't want to be seen risking loot on their
own horses. The only trouble with the system was that I
had to limit myself to five and ten-dollar bets or I'd be
knocking the odds down too low, but even so I netted
about five hundred dollars for the weekend.

My one notable failure was in the sixth on the last day
with a scrawny filly belonging to a sheriff from Montana
who was known to me only as Boyo and looked as if he'd
just been sent over for the part from Central Casting. He
had a blimp-sized stomach, hands like rusty buckets and a
complexion resembling a railroad map painted in purple.
"Son," Boyo told me, "this filly of mine has a world of
speed, but she quits like a dawg. Today, son, she ain't
gonna quit. Here's twenty dollars. Run it through a bit at a
time and come see me after the race, you hear?"

I heard and also bet ten dollars of my own on her. The
race went off and, sure enough, Boyo's nag opened up
seven or eight lengths. On the turn for home she started
to shorten stride, then, just as the field caught up to her,
she began to buck and threw her jockey.

I caught up to Boyo later. He was leaning against a wall
behind the stands, looking disconsolate. I asked him what
had happened. "Aw," he said, "she didn't like that buzzer
none."

A couple of days after Cespedes was suspended, I went
partying with some friends and found myself sitting briefly
alone late at night in a corner of a bar at a ramshackle
establishment right on the water that served up mediocre
but expensive food and drink, as well as music by some
combo that had not yet learned how to hold a steady beat
but did occasionally raise the roof. I was very tired and
ready to leave, but before I could go my old friend Sam
the Cynic spotted me from the bar, came over, and sat
down. We smiled at each other and waited for the band
to take a much-needed break.

"So what do you think?" Sam asked, during a lull in the uproar.

"Think about what, Sam?"

"This thing about Cespedes getting five days," he explained. "I think he shoulda gotten months, not days."

"Why? The stewards think the goad is useless."

"The stewards know better than that," Sam said. "Let's say you hit a horse with juice in the morning, when nobody's looking. Now the horse gets out on the track, runs a bit, then gets jolted. It stands to reason, don't it, that when you touch him there on the neck during a race, the horse don't know you ain't got a live battery? He thinks he's about to be jolted again and he takes off. OK, some pigs wouldn't run if you was to wrap 'em up in high-tension wires or prick 'em in the balls. But some horses, especially the quitters, they'll give you that second effort. Now I'm not saying that's what Cespedes did, and anyway his horse don't win, but the thing is, if your horse is conditioned to juice and you know it'll make him put out, then using a goad makes sense. I'd have given Cespedes months, not days."

Sam never sees the positive side of any question and always assumes the worst, but there are times when I can listen to him with more than casual interest. Anyway, by this time I was a pretty sure loser for the whole meet and had a good healthy paranoia going. Sam was the sort of man who could feed it and keep it well. In fact, for two whole days after that night I went to the races but didn't make a bet.

19

Sweet Dreams

I was up in the guinea stand one morning when Viva La Vivi cantered by, after working an easy three furlongs. I recognized her immediately and not just because her trainer Harold Hodosh, who was with her, is a friend of mine. I saw her run her first race and I've followed her career ever since. She's one of my favorite horses, a big running fool of a mare with the disposition of a lap dog. I once stood outside her stall while Harold fed her her morning coffee, which she takes with plenty of cream, and Eddie, her groom, told me she was the nicest mare he'd ever handled. She walks with her head down and gets so bored with the backside routine that she looks asleep most of the time. But take her out on the track and she becomes a tiger, about as tough a race mare as there is at sprint distances. "She doesn't like anybody to get in front of her," Janie once explained to me. "She hates to have all that dirt kicked up in her face. That's because she's really fastidious. If she gets all dirty and like that, she'll come back looking so disgusted and everything." Janie has her own way of looking at things, but she may be right, I wouldn't know. When Vivi runs and Janie's at the track to bet on her, I don't even look at the *Form* or the odds; I just go to the windows and buy tickets. Vivi rarely disappoints me.

I'd seen Vivi run before I met Janie, but I hadn't known much about her until Janie took me to see her one day at Santa Anita. Janie stood outside her stall and petted her and talked to her, addressing her exclusively as "sweetheart." No one loves this mare more than Janie, except, perhaps, for Hodosh; Vivi was Harold's first really good horse and the trainer, who grew up in Poland and had to get out when the Nazis took over during World War II, quite understandably rates all of his horses above most of the people he knows. "I first saw her when she was two and Harold had just brought her to the track," Janie told me. "She was so sweet and good-looking, but too docile, everybody said. They meant she didn't have enough spirit in her to be a racehorse. Oh, my goodness, were they ever wrong! But Harold knew. I was dating a friend of his at the time and Harold had told him all about the horse. God, if it hadn't been for this horse, I might still be broke and owing everybody and just miserable and all!"

Janie is a cute little redhead with freckles and big green eyes and, though now in her mid-thirties, doesn't look a day over fourteen. She used to sit with a group of friends in a box next to mine at Santa Anita and at first I thought she was somebody's precocious daughter. Later, after I was introduced to her, I got the idea she was somebody's wife. She had been, of course, but the marriage had broken up some months before in a great mushroom cloud of bad checks and unpaid bills, the result of her husband's fatal predilection for heavy gambling weekends in Las Vegas and nights at the Gardena poker parlors, and when I met her she was dating a jockey's agent. I gathered it wasn't serious, but it didn't matter to me at the time. My own marriage had ended and a subsequent long relationship with another woman had just broken up and I was in no mood for further entanglements. Janie and I became racetrack friends and talked horses.

It turned out that we had both been at the track for Vivi's maiden race and had won on her, though she'd paid less than even money. "I bet ten dollars on her that day," Janie told me, "but I had to borrow four dollars to do it. It was a fortune to me. That was what my life was like then. Marvin owed money everywhere and, because we were still legally married, the creditors were chasing both of us." They'd garnisheed her salary twice and once a pair of IRS agents came to dun her in the office where she worked as receptionist and bookkeeper for three swinging Beverly Hills psychiatrists. "It was just a nightmare," she recalled. "That's how I got involved in racing. It was an escape. Two of my doctors owned a piece of a horse that Harold trained and they took me to the track. I'd never been before, though I grew up in Wyoming and knew about horses and all. But I'd never seen a horse race, much less bet money on one."

She immediately began to have these strange dreams. "The first horse dream I ever had," she recalled, "was about one of my doctors coming to my house. He had an emergency case at the hospital and he asked me to bet five dollars for him on a horse called Prince O'Pace that 'couldn't lose,' he said." She reported this dream the next morning to her employers, but no such horse was listed in the entries that day at any track and no one had ever heard of the animal. But about ten days later the name popped up in the *Form* as one of the longshots in that day's feature race at Hollywood Park. Everyone in the office, even two of the patients, got down on it and Prince O'Pace won, paying $29.80. "I had ten dollars on it," Janie said. "God, we just about broke that poor bookie!"

She had another dream about a horse called Selecting. The race was run at six furlongs and Selecting was number two. He was last out of the gate, then went wide on the turn, looped the field and won. Selecting, a horse Janie had never heard of before, ran about a week later and at six furlongs, but he wore the number seven. "That worried me and worried me," Janie said, "because, in the dream, I'd seen the number two, so I didn't know whether to bet or not. I finally put five dollars on him." Selecting won exactly as she had dreamed it and paid thirteen dollars. "Golly, you know how nearsighted you are," Betsy, the other girl in the office, told her. "Two looks like seven, if you aren't wearing glasses, doesn't it?"

The doctors had a little filly named Volanoor and so far she'd had no luck. In her first race for them she'd been so badly ridden by her jockey that Harold had smashed his fist into the side of their box when she ran her heart out and came in third in a race everyone felt she should have one. A couple of weeks later Harold entered her again and put Laffit Pincay, one of the best riders in the world, on her back. Janie hadn't dreamed about the first race, but she had a good one this time. She was at the track and standing in the winner's circle next to the horse, with Phyllis, one of the doctor's wives, beside her. The doctor himself came running up at the last minute and wedged himself between the two women. She dreamed nothing about the race itself.

It was a slow day at the office, with a couple of cancellations, and Jane and Betsy and all the doctors and their wives rushed out to the track in mid-afternoon to see Volanoor run. She won and Janie scrambled down to the winner's circle with nine or ten other people and everything happened exactly as in her dream. "You see, it's just like Janie dreamed it," one of the doctors told Harold. "The hair just stood right up on the back of my arms," Janie remembered.

One of Janie's dreams puzzled her at first. She was in the laundry room of her apartment building and all the machines were going and Laffit Pincay came in. He helped her put the soap in the washers and folded her clothes for her and just couldn't have been nicer. When Janie told everyone at work about this dream, no one could figure out what it meant, not even the two Freudians. But her jockey's agent, whom she'd just begun dating, had a plausible interpretation. "It means Pincay is going to help you clean up," he explained. So, on the following Saturday, Janie went out to Santa Anita and bet Pincay to win in every race. "It was the day Laffit won six races," she said, "and only about two of them were favorites. I should have parlayed my winnings, but I was scared. I had so little money of my own. In fact, I was living on what I won at the track with these dreams, because just about everything I made in my job was going to help pay off Marvin's creditors. We owed over ten thousand dollars at one time."

It was Viva La Vivi who finally got her out. The filly won her first three races with Janie's money on her, after which Harold gave her a rest. In her next race Janie bet thirty dollars on her and she won again. "The only time I lost on her," Janie remembered, "was a race in which she had a lot of trouble and came in third, but one day she paid $16.80 and I had her across the board. It just seemed that Vivi was lucky for me, even though I hadn't yet had a dream about her. Every weekend I'd go out to Harold's barn to see her and talk to her. My whole life began to center on this horse. I just had a feeling about her that I couldn't explain."

One day Janie went out to Santa Anita and bought a Daily Double ticket on her two lucky numbers that year, four and seven, and it hit for $147.80. "I was sitting there in the box when, along about the third race, Harold and his brother Stewart came by and I offered to buy them a drink with my winnings," she said, "but they knew about my situation and all and they wouldn't let me. Then, along about the fifth race, they told me Vivi was running in a stakes race on the following Wednesday. I knew I had to come to that one and I could, because it was a Wednesday and the office was closed in the afternoon."

And then Janie had her first dream about Vivi. The race was at six and a half furlongs on the downhill turf course and Janie couldn't tell who was riding her, but Vivi was on the outside and going head and head with a horse called Impressive Style and eventually she pulled away to win by a neck. "I also dreamt that she hurt her leg," Janie recalled, "but I didn't tell that part of the dream to anyone. I was sick about it."

On the Wednesday of the race, Janie put on her best dress, put all the money she had in the world, a hundred and forty-eight dollars, in her purse and drove out to the track feeling sick to her stomach from fright. At the paddock, before the race, she ran into Stewart, who was all dressed up in a beautiful suit and tie. "I couldn't believe it," Janie said. "It was all just right. I'd never seen Stewart in a suit before. He usually wore old clothes to the track." He put his arms around her and told her that Vivi would win.

Janie made three separate trips to the five-dollar windows and bet all but eight dollars of her money on the horse to win. Just before post time she got up and went back to a two-dollar window and bet another four dollars on Vivi to win and then, inexplicably, two dollars on her to place. She went back to her seat clutching her purse; she had exactly $2.17 left. "It's the closest I ever came to fainting at the racetrack, I was so terrified," she recalled. "That kind of money meant so much to me."

Viva La Vivi won exactly as she had in Janie's dream, coming on the outside to edge Impressive Style by a neck. She paid better than five to one. In the winner's circle, while they were all getting their pictures taken, Janie noticed that one of Vivi's back legs was bleeding, but Harold assured her it was nothing serious, just a superficial cut from one of her own hooves. "I cried all the way back to my seat. Then I took my money home and hid it and the next day I opened a savings account under another name."

I've seen quite a lot of Janie over the past few months since she first told me this story and we have become more than friends. She's getting a divorce and her money troubles are over. She still goes to the track and bets a few dollars every now and then, usually only on horses she has strong personal feelings about. Now that she no longer needs them, the dreams have stopped, much to everyone's dismay, but we're all still hoping they'll start again. If they ever do, I won't have to buy a *Form* to pick my winners.

Viva La Vivi did not run last summer at Del Mar. Harold gave her the summer off and got ready to take her East, with the idea of running her in the fall at Belmont and Aqueduct in New York. In the spring she'd be retired and bred to Secretariat. When her first foal is ready to come to the races, I hope Janie and I will be there to help Harold's own sweet dream come true.

20

Saturation Point

I can pinpoint exactly the day I knew I had had enough of Del Mar. It was on August 26, a Tuesday, when the horsemen held something called a Sports Spectacular. The events included a Celebrity Tennis Classic, to be held at eleven A.M. at the Lodge, and the Sixth Annual Bacharach-Shoemaker Basketball Game, to be contested that evening in Bing Crosby Hall, the main exhibition building a couple of hundred yards behind the grandstand. All proceeds from the games, as well as an informal afternoon picnic to be given in the track infield, were to go to a fund "to build a permanent home for needy horsemen." The annual event, now in its sixth year, had so far raised over fifty thousand dollars for what is undoubtedly a worthy cause. I had no argument with it and the events themselves turned out to be moderately entertaining. It was simply that, without knowing it, I had suddenly and unexpectedly had enough of horses and horse people to last me—well, a couple of

months at least. I longed to be back home, in front of my
fireplace and with a Verdi opera on the hi-fi and the occasional sound of a human voice discussing something, anything, as long as it was totally unconnected to horse racing.
I had never imagined I could reach such a time, but I had
and it definitely had very little to do with the fact that I
was a loser for the meet. I had cut my betting way down,
in fact, and was actually holding my own. No, my satura-
tion point simply came because I am not a professional
horseman, I could never be completely inside their world,
and, furthermore, I had discovered I didn't want to be.

I think this realization struck me very forcibly on Sports
Spectacular Day because, for the first time, I saw the horsemen outside of their world and performing like amateurs
in unfamiliar surroundings. The only jockey, for instance,
who could play tennis even adequately was Bill Shoemaker. He has no overhead, but plays a graceful, studied
game, with a sure touch on his lob. Even so, he was the
weakest of the four players in the featured match of the
morning, which pitted him and an aging vet named Jim
Temple, who used to be ranked, against trainer Chay
Knight and Desi Arnaz, Jr., both erratic but big hitters.
Knight and Arnaz won 9–7, which caused a familiar voice
in back of me to begin cursing. "Sonofabitch," he said, "if
it ain't just like at the track! I bet him there and he don't
win either. And if I *don't* bet him, he kills me!"

The rest of the tennis was pretty miserable, with only a
couple of the trainers and owners showing any ability to
hit the ball. Of course, actor Jack Klugman had prepared
us for this eventuality with a graceful little introduction to
the tournament. "You're not going to see Stan Smith or

Jimmy Connors here," he told the roughly three hundred
people who showed up at the Lodge courts. "You *are* going
to see good horsemen playing hard. And we're going to
root for them, just as we root for their losing horses." The
morning might have been more entertaining if some of the
celebrities announced for the event—James Caan, Telly
Savalas, Don Adams, and Burt Bacharach—had been able
to show up, but on the whole no one was overly disap-
pointed. When the tennis got too boring, I left and walked
around in the sunshine, while between matches a rock
band composed of about a dozen repulsively precocious
children massacred "California Dreamin' " and some other
good songs.

I skipped the picnic in the afternoon, but showed up at
Bing Crosby Hall for the basketball game. To my surprise,
it was played for real, by which I mean that the two
pick-up teams from the backside captained by Shoemaker
and the absent Bacharach really went at each other. Two
or three of the players, most notably one of the black
grooms, had obviously played the game well, but after a
while it, too, became a study in ineptitude. At half-time, a
team of Del Mar jockeys took on some airline stewardesses
in an abbreviated game refereed by some clown who
slapped the jockeys with more fouls than any of them had
received in their entire riding careers. Mary Bacon, looking
adorable in very brief shorts, played for the jockeys, but
the referee ignored her and wooed the other eleven girls.
It was all in fun, of course. I think the stewardesses won,
but I can't be sure because by that time I began to feel
I'd been somehow locked into a typically plastic media

event of the sort one sees usually emanating from Las
Vegas. I got up long before the proceedings ended and
went back to my room.

That room! I had never known before what it was like
to have to live in a cheap motel room for nearly two
months. I stood briefly in the doorway and stared around
at the lugubrious waiting-room furniture, the barren walls,
the great glass eye of the television set staring emptily toward the bed. In the half-open closet my summer clothes
hung lopsidedly on wire hangers. Old *Racing Forms* and
programs and lined yellow note pads squatted sullenly on
a tiny desk crowded between my bed and a couch, on
which reposed my typewriter and a mound of old under-
wear and socks. Against the gray plastic drapes drawn
across double glass doors looking directly out into a parking lot beat an orange glow from electric signs advertising
gas stations and eating places up the road by the freeway
ramps. I went into the bathroom, where every day the
Mexican maids wrapped my drinking glasses in wax paper
and looped a sanitation certificate around my toilet seat,
while neglecting either to sweep the floor or scrub the tub.
A pile of old threadbare towels huddled in one corner and
a leak from the faucet had crept the full length of the sink
to drench my toilet articles.

I decided I didn't want to go to bed in this room that
night and then I realized that this was how most of the
horse people lived all year round. Not the establishment
bunch or the rich owners or the relatively few people
really making it, but the vast majority of the backside help.
Actually, my quarters were luxurious compared to theirs;

I knew men who hadn't lived in homes of their own for years, but bunked down every night in tiny airless cubicles over the stables or in cabins erected between the rows of barns, the living quarters provided free by the racetracks and comparable in every way to those available to all migratory workers, only worse than most. What the back-side people need is a Chavez. I told myself I was being a fool, but a huge, miasmic depression slowly began to settle in for the duration. I went out and bought a pint of Jack Daniels and drove down to the beach and sat alone on the sand and drank most of it. Then I drove very carefully back to the Lodge and managed at last to get to bed.

I was awakened several times during the night by the sound of love-making in the next room. Some obviously enamored couple were getting it on. I could hear every-thing, because the walls of my room were, for all I know, built out of soda crackers and Swiss cheese. "Oh God, oh God," the woman kept moaning, "you're the greatest, baby, you're the best! Oh, Jesus, no one ever did me like you before! God, what a stud you are, sweetheart! What a king! Give it to me again, lover!"

I wasn't about to interrupt the king at his manly court-ship. Oh, no. I'm no spoilsport. So I'd wake up and lie there and listen, then drift back to sleep. But the last time I woke up it was because some other woman was out in the hallway pounding on the king's door. "Lou Ann, Lou Ann!" she said. "Get your ass out of there! You ain't sup-posed to stay more than an hour with him! Lou Ann, you hear me? Thirty-five bucks don't buy more than an hour!"

"Shut the fuck up, I'm comin'" Lou Ann answered.

"Where's my money, sport?"

The king mumbled something and five minutes later I heard his door slam. I went back to sleep and didn't wake up again. I can always relax in classy surroundings.

21

Getaway Day

The season finally ended on Wednesday, September 10, with the twenty-eighth running of the Del Mar Futurity, a mile race for two-year-olds that was won by Telly's Pop, the first horse ever owned by Telly Savalas of "Kojak" fame and a movie producer named Howard Koch. It wasn't much of a contest, really, because the other two-year-olds this year were an undistinguished lot and Telly's Pop romped home. The race I was interested in was the last one, in which an old plater named Montana Winds was trying to post his fifth victory of the meet, which would have set a new record for a single season at Del Mar. He was going at a mile and three-eighths on the turf and against slightly better horses than he'd been beating. He was the second choice of the bettors and I didn't think he could win, because the distance was just a little farther than he likes to run, but I was rooting for him all the same. I knew the horse and the trainer, Tom Blincoe, and I liked them both.

After Montana Winds had won his fourth consecutive race at Del Mar, I'd gone around with Barry Irwin to Blincoe's barn to talk to him. The trainer wasn't there, but Barry introduced me to the horse's owner, a middle-aged heavyset man named Floyd Elkus, whom we found hanging around the stable. He was attired in a smartly tailored leisure suit and a good deal of heavy gold jewelry and he was absolutely delighted to hear we were interested in his animal. "I just wanted a horse to have some fun with," he explained in a voice like a ruptured trombone. "I used to be in the rag business, but I retired and I was looking around for something to do."

He was at Hollywood Park on June 4 with his friend Frank Costello, a retired contractor for whom Blincoe trained a few horses, when Montana Winds came out on the track to run in a cheap claiming race. Costello had taken the horse on Blincoe's say-so a few months earlier, but the eight-year-old gelding had failed to score in eight outings. In fact, he'd lost his last four for Costello by an average margin of fourteen lengths. "If this horse doesn't run one–two–three today I'm going to ship him to Caliente," Costello told Elkus.

"What do you want to send a nice old horse like that to Caliente for?" Elkus asked and offered to buy him.

Costello agreed on the spot. He'd originally paid eight thousand for the horse, but told Elkus he'd let him go for the price of his claiming tag that day, sixty-two hundred and fifty dollars. He also offered to throw in half of whatever share of the purse Montana Winds might win and stipulated that he had to finish sound. "It was an offer I couldn't refuse," Elkus recalled, "and we shook hands on it just as Tom and his wife arrived. So Frank turns to Tom and very grandly he informs him that 'Montana Winds is no longer in *my* stable, he's in Mr. *Elkus'* stable!' "

Montana Winds ran second that day, after leading most of the way around the track, and was not claimed. Elkus handed Costello a check on the spot for fifty-eight hundred dollars, which represented the claiming price minus half the purse for the second-place finish. "Tom looked at me kind of strange after the race," Elkus remembered. "Later I got to talking to Tom and he told me that of all the horses he'd claimed for Frank, only Montana Winds and one other had been his idea."

The first race Montana Winds ever ran for Elkus was a bad one, but the self-styled rag merchant wasn't discouraged. "I knew this horse would come around," he explained. "He'd had all kinds of problems but he'd been a stakes horse at one time and I wasn't about to see him sent down the river. He had too much class."

When the racing moved to Del Mar, Blincoe put Milo Valenzuela up on the horse and Montana Winds took off on his winning streak. Elkus was delighted, because he felt that Montana Winds and Milo were made for each other. "They're both classy old campaigners, two old champions, making comebacks," he said. "I looked up my horse's lifetime record after his last race and did you know that was his twentieth win in sixty-four starts and that he's earned just about a hundred thousand? Also, it was the third time he'd won at least three in a row in his career. What I'm most pleased about, though, is that this has given Milo a chance to get his name in the limelight once again."

I'd heard something about Valenzuela's troubles. He'd

been a favorite of mine back East, especially after inheriting the mount on Kelso when Arcaro retired. He'd also been the finest rider of young, green horses I'd ever seen, but there had been rumors even then of epic bouts with the bottle and, since coming west a few years ago, he'd ridden only sporadically. A lot of trainers wouldn't use him because he reportedly couldn't be counted on even to show up for the race, much less an early-morning workout. "Milo? He's always an hour late and a dollar short," one trainer had told me. He'd been riding well at Del Mar, but the California Highway Patrol had picked him up one day, after watching him weave at high speeds all over the road, and Elkus had had to offer to put up bail to get him out of stir. "I'll get him and lock him in his room, if I have to," he said. "I want Milo up on my horse every time he runs."

I asked Elkus if he'd seen much of Costello since that day at Hollywood Park. "Well, sure," Elkus said. "I had to thank him, didn't I? I've made twelve thousand in purses off the horse. And you know what Frank says to me? 'I'm glad you got him,' he says, 'because if he went bad again and had to be retired, I'd have to bring him to my ranch and watch him do that dancing.' Montana Winds is what they call a weaver. He dances back and forth all day long in his stall. Frank only likes nice, quiet horses, not dancers."

Montana Winds made a brave try in the ninth on closing day. He gave weight to every other horse in the race and went out on the lead, his preferred running style. Another speed horse called Hook and Eye forced the pace, then fell back and several others made a run at Montana Winds, but at the head of the stretch he was still in front. He "shook off challengers to set the pace," according to the *Form*, but tired toward the end and finished fourth, beaten by less than two lengths. It was as gutsy a performance as I'd seen all summer.

The boys up in the press box voted a three-year-old named Larrikin the Horse of the Meeting, for having won two big turf races in record-breaking style, and other meaningless honors were awarded to stakes and handicap horses in various divisions. Frankel was voted the best trainer, presumably because he'd won the most races. These elections, held toward the end of every race meet, never fail to reflect the obvious—important races won, money earned, records broken. I'd have voted for Montana Winds and maybe Tom Blincoe and so, I suspect, would most of the two-dollar bettors, but then nobody ever asks them anything.

I walked out of Del Mar for the last time after the ninth race and I really had no regrets. I'd lost a total of about nine hundred dollars for the seven weeks of betting, but then that was to be expected. In all forms of gambling it is impossible to win consistently and I know of no one who does, though I'd been stupid to lose as much as I had in the early part of the meeting. The trouble was, I told myself, that Hollywood Park had been too kind to me and I'd been overconfident. I didn't think I'd make that mistake again, though it had taken a long time and some notable disappointments to convince me. No, I had no regrets. For years I'd wanted to follow one race meeting all the way through *à la Hemingway* from start to finish and I had. I'd also found out at last that horse racing was a world I did not belong in as a regular and that, too, I could only have learned by saturating myself in it. I didn't think I would ever run away to it again, as I had once or twice before in my life.

If the racetrack is anything to me and to most of the people I know, it's an escape, a refuge from the mundane world of bills and personal problems and disasters, large and small, of all sorts. As you sit there and the horses come out onto the track, there is only one reality beyond the beauty of the spectacle itself and that is the outcome of the race and your ability to predict it, as confirmed by the risk of money on the line. There is no thrill quite like it and it will continue, I know, to lure me back again and again, though never to engulf me totally.

The track is a dismal place to leave on getaway day. You shuffle out through a sea of trash, knowing it's all over, remembering all the right decisions but also all the wrong ones you may have made, and the music that sounded so sweet weeks before fades now in your ears as you go. I walked back to my motel through the stable area. I glanced back once at the grandstand. Papers blew about the empty seats and already the work crews were busy cleaning up. The course itself was deserted now and would remain that way for months, until next year when the big vans would begin moving south again.

Most of the horses had gone, too, by this time. Row after row of stalls gaped emptily at me as I strolled past. Two big vans were loading not far from the racing office and I could hear one of the men cursing as an animal quite sensibly resisted being pushed inside. A chilly breeze stirred up clouds of dust and blew them between the shed rows of what would soon be a ghost town. The horse people were moving on, taking their travelling circus to the next city, where every day would be a new beginning and the routine cycle of the race meet, with all its familiar hopes and dreams and joys and crushing disappointments, would be repeated once again, as inevitably and predictably as the turning of the seasons.

I had already packed and there were no goodbyes to be said. We were all leaving. I quickly loaded my suitcases into my car and drove north again with the horses.